The Beast is We

By

Dennis Cruz

Punk ⚕ Hostage ⚕ Press

The Beast is We

ISBN 978-1-940213-04-0

Punk Hostage Press
punkhostagepress.com

Editor: Iris Berry

Introduction: Richard Modiano

Cover Design: Dennis Cruz / Chilandia

Back Cover Photo: Dennis Cruz

Introduction

Like the segments of a scorpion's tail *The Beast is We* is divided into six parts, each leading inexorably to the stinger *0,* each segment introduced with a prose poem.

Along the way Dennis Cruz brings the reader into a reality that is rendered potent by the process of its creation, the way in which the poet's imagination is given form and directed toward an end. It is both a quotidian reality drawn from the poet's life and a philosophical reality that Cruz creates and into which he gives himself birth. Cruz not only shares his own reality, but also imposes it at will upon the reader, and his ability to control this imaginative universe extends also to the appearances perceived by others in the act of reading the poem.

The poems reveal the workings of a subtle intelligence and a painfully open sensibility. The vivid particulars make the poems immediate and are part of a larger awareness of the mental space in which they are birthed, suggesting a greater (or deeper) universe than the small circle of ordinary consciousness: "a little man/in Peru/shaving the/bark/from a root/tossing things/into a boiling pot/infusing the fire/with heavy/prayer/and deep breath/chanting…" The mind of the poet, his specific thoughts, his changing moods, is shown to exist within and act within the larger human and non-human universe.

This examination of mind is not the "egotistical sublime" of the Romantic poets since it pays attention to levels of consciousness that exist beyond ego, and the flashes of dead pan humor draw attention to the fictive nature of ego itself. The poetry is at turns playful, melancholy and astonished at the fact of existing as part of this fundamentally weird universe. Cruz's poetry interrogates the transformations of consciousness, how objective reality is created by and creates the mind of the poet, and it does so with wit, elegance, subtlety and sharp humor.

The emotions are built deep into the lines, each line poignantly tense, with awe, grief, regret, terror, beauty, the syntactic elements releasing the flow of emotions, images, ideas and sound, reality in its dynamic sense proceeding from an interior state, nurtured by what we call imagination, and brought to an exterior existence that is alive and perpetually moving.

Cruz, poet and singer, creative, receptive and sensitive, knows about the essentiality of form in word and sound, in the visible and the tangible. He does not disdain what appears small or insignificant, because he sees the great in the small. The sounds and signs of which this poetry is formed, become the vehicles of meaningful forces. Through them the visible takes on the nature of symbols, the tangible becomes a creative tool of the spirit, and life becomes a deep stream, flowing from eternity to eternity.

The Beast is We is a dense, erudite, wide ranging collection couched in the language of every day speech that has been transformed by the poet Dennis Cruz into language that is magical, visionary and brutal in its unflinching look at the reality of being human.

- Richard Modiano
Executive Director
Beyond Baroque Literary Arts Center
Venice, CA

Table of Contents

2.

1.

"when they shall have finished their testimony, the beast that ascendeth out of the bottomless pit shall make war against them, and shall overcome them and kill them."

Revelation 11:7
The New Testament
King James Version

6

black water

it was terrible, the river that couldn't be there, there where streets used to run, up against the buildings and it's too deep and doesn't belong, and because of the water the lights don't work and without city lights the buildings become like giant tombstones and looking up at them from the too wrong canoe I shouldn't /can't be riding in, it's terror, pure and clean and the moonlight shafts between the buildings but it's too bright because the tombstone towers have brought the night to more darkness than it's used to. and I know I'm going to a party but I don't want to because the terror, somewhere in Boyle Heights, I'm sure it's in Boyle Heights but it's an art party and I don't care for fancy people and I know there is nothing to do with art at an art party and I know I'll have to get to and explain the severed head later because it was floating and talking but when we got to the party and had to tie off the canoe to some stairway railing I kept looking back at how strange it was that the city was covered in water and the lights were gone and I worried there might be excrement in the water but I couldn't see in the dark and I couldn't smell anything but fog.

then in the party, the giant loft with pristine white walls and 20 foot ceilings and red lamps and the room, the elevated room, off to the side like a stage or performance space, and everyone talking there and laughing and me sensing something was happening there but what? so wandering over of course and the very tall brunette with dark red lipstick and the clinging cocktail dress with the diamond studded bracelet that was actually the end of a very fancy leash and I follow the jewels on the leash down to the pet. and the pet was a naked native American Indian man, crouching down on all fours, I could see his penis dangling as he brought his face down to a bowl of water on the floor. and no one in that room was looking at him, they just kept on talking and laughing and whispering conspiratorial nothings at each other and everyone looked so important and precious, but I couldn't take my eyes off of his and he looked at me too and the sadness was huge and no one cared and I heard the tall lady say: they're so awesome, you really have to get yourself one.

and I don't think the severed head floating just above the tip of the canoe was my mother but now when I try to remember it I keep suspecting that it was because it was terrifying and certain kinds of terror always lead to her and how she died and why and why and why but the head was talking and kind of laughing maybe telling us where to go maybe telling us we shouldn't go I don't remember anymore but it was bigger than a head should be like twice as big maybe and it was bright and easy to see even though the street rivers were dark because downtown was underwater and it looked like rot and I thought: how long has the city been flooded and when did we lose the streets? and if it was a dream like that I don't want to dream like that because it's me and what I see and I don't want to translate because it will lead back to me all of it, the slave on a leash and the dark of the city......just wondering what's under all that black water....I can't think about it...I just can't think about that because I will unravel and I really need to keep it together.

irrational

I was seven
years old
and deathly afraid
of insects.
my uncle
knew this.
one day
he caught
a grasshopper
and ripped off
it's front legs
with his fingers.
he showed it to me
still wriggling
in his dirty hands.
he saw how
afraid of it
I was
and a slow smile
spread across
his face
next thing you know
I was running
and he was laughing
and...
coming after me.
something
about how
he was going
to make me
eat it.
I wish I could say
he never
caught me
but ...

with them

the reasons
are coming

that sweet
dead dog
in the street
that looked like
it was
just sleeping
eyes open
and looking
into mine

the reasons
there in the
leaves
their trees
offering
no explanation
other than
they're trees
and so are we

heart
holding heavy
bags,
waiting for
the bus

why I was
crying,
why I didn't
investigate.
just let the tears
be about
whatever they
wanted

a little man
in Peru
shaving the
bark
from a root
tossing things
into a boiling pot
infusing the fire
with heavy
prayer
and deep breath
chanting

reasons
there in
my curiosity

closing the
outside
of my eyes
so they can
open
inside
and no surprise
to find
walls
of eyes
seeing me
see them

the reasons
coming
dressed in
revelation
and the
slutty
make up
of excuses
smeared

the reasons
are
coming
and I'm
coming
with them.

so many days

sure,
in this context
sure,
because it wasn't
every day
that we ate
THAT much acid.
and it wasn't the radio
that turned the car
into what the car
turned into
but it did have
something to do with
radio waves.
didn't it?
I think it did.
and we turned,
mirrored up
all the while acting,
like we weren't even
tripping.
then spent
years and years
like that,
didn't we?
I think we did.
It wasn't
every day,
but probably
a lot of days,
I mean
so many
fucking days

sacred dark

smoking
pulling
in the sickness
a tiny respite
from obey
or else
silent
in respect of
what precious
words
remain

my caged beast
singing
a sickening
blues

roaches
scuttling
eyes looking out
the dark
ape-caves
of my remembering

and you
with your
cadaver
catheter
smile
you
with your
costume
delivery
and casket
charm

taunting,
luring

and condemning
as always
your eyes
glinting
with lineage

years
of looking
away
looking
in

my eyes
closing
to sacred
dark

seeding myself
there
growing
someone
there.

quietly knowing

oh what a labyrinth
we've made
for our souls
one self
after another
lost in the maze
of our self
deprecations
guilty because
we knew,
and did nothing
lost as we were
in our own
powerful delusions
choosing the
weakest version
of a constantly
shifting reality
because we were
young once,
because we thought
we understood
- the world.
how wrong we were
knowing now
there is no
understanding
only knowing,
quietly knowing
and powerless
to change,
anything,
but our
perspective.

no translation

perhaps we could
with our fingers
turning red
and turning
away from
being fingers

perhaps we could
with our eyes
finally closed
busily helping
the ears

and then
we do
with our
hearts out
and our
heads
open in
space

awash
in knowing
something
sleeping
in our blood

not scientists
not preachers
not tyrants
not prophets
not chosen
not blind
not even
eyes

no one

can explain
how your
mouth
closes,
with
last words
on *its* tongue

a symphony
of regret
so many
things
left
unsaid

things
I need
to say

even if it
kills me

even
after

it kills
me.

bad, bad news

one foot
swelling
pulling out
of a fight

a dark tree

remembering
trying not
to let it go
a wet wing
heavy with blood
two lives sliding
back into
the land
of the living

her shoulder
leaning down
into her knee
a cramp spreading
her eyes scanning
the room

her regalia
rustling
in the dark
making her way
to the bathroom
and back to the
bed

so late
it's early

her wrist
opening, bleeding
broken promises

the night of her
heart beating,
the morning
of all of her
stopping

and the inevitable
phone calls
all the pertinent
people alerted
the next
of kin
the gods
within

waking
heavy
feet across
chipping
kitchen tile
still
rooted
in last night's
dream

morning dew
the eyes of you

oh baby
your mother's
gone
she died baby
I'm so sorry

hilarious

in the end
what matters
most
is not
what happened
to you
but more,
what you think
and believe
happened

this is why
I believe
perspective
is more
important
than love
or hope

because
without it
incest jokes
just wouldn't
be
funny.

absent

you look so much
like your father
that motherfucker
you want to be a clown
all your life?
you're just
like your father.
everything's
a fucking joke
to you.
a real comedian.
your father
was a piece of shit
you know that?
oh yeah?
you want new pants?
call your
fucking father
here's the phone
no it's ringing
ask your fucking father
for new pants.
let's see if he even
remembers you.
oh, he didn't
pick up?
fuck him,
come here,
why are you crying?
oh, you're going
to cry now?
you want to cry?
I'm the one
that should be
crying

and then

first my ears
bowl up
and wrap around
the headphones
like big wet
clamshells

then the tones
start bending
I mean serious
multi-dimensional
bending

then my fingers
start to grow,
turning into long
sinewy
graceful
branches

and then my feet
root down
into the earth
and with the art
pumping blood
into my heart
the soul of me
gets to swimming

first in the
lake
and then
when the light dims
the ocean.

so much music
knowing
suddenly

the church of it,
the sanctuary
of it

then my eyes
open to a room
of eyes opening

and I can see
what they see
feel what they feel

and so much
of it
is *me.*

and then my
blood
reddens
my eyes

and I can
finally
see

you
right there
next to
US

sorcery

"you wanna see a trick?"
of course I said yes,
I was eight, who doesn't
want to see a trick when
they're eight? He was nine
cause he got held back
so of course I looked up to him,
and he was taller
than everyone else
in my class.
we were walking home
from school, on Olympic Blvd.,
I lived on Normandie
and we were just a couple
blocks from my house.
"check this out…" he said
with his eyes shining and his teeth
bared in this menacing grin.
he then pulled his pants down,
bent over, and opened his two
ass cheeks with his hands.
I had never seen an asshole
opened up like that before
so I thought: not bad, but that's
no trick. Suddenly it began
to open, and a monstrous log
of a turd came sliding out.
It was fucking amazing.
I had no idea an asshole could
open so wide. It was the most
amazing thing I had ever seen.
I almost threw up.
then just like that it was over
and he just pulled his pants up
and started walking, giggling like
he had just shown me some funny
secret thing
that's when I knew

he was fucking crazy.
not crazy like he was wild
or brave
but the other kind of crazy.
the *eating cockroaches*
while jacking off
kind of crazy.
after that,
I was always afraid
of being alone with him.
I knew his older brother
was a friend of my uncles
and word on the street was
he was crazy too.
I never could figure out
how he thought
taking a shit on the sidewalk
while holding your ass open
with your hands
was a trick,
but now that I'm older
I can appreciate
the magic in it, I mean
it's definitely black magic,
but I get it now.
the fact that I never forgot about it
really says something.
I'm not sure what it says, but man
I wonder where Carlos is now?
I wonder what he turned out
to be like?
whatever he is,
I'll bet he's at least
interesting.

smiley

you were going to be
the man with the tall glass
always with the
slight smile
conveying
nothing.
you were going to be
because I expected
it from you
I see now,
that I was
wrong.
I see now
that no one
can ever be
a perfect projection.
still, after all this
time
I sometimes
wait
at the end of
some bar
hoping to
see you there
sliding over
that tall glass
smirking with that
tiny smile,
the smile
that never
denoted
anything.

home is where the _____ is

of course
I love you
with your nipples
in my mouth
and your ass
grinding
on my lap

and what does it
matter,
the source
of my devotion?

so long as I
don't stray
too far
from whatever
part of you
I choose
to call
my home.

destination

at some point
you have to
pick a side,
you have to
make a
choice.
you can't
linger
on the fence
forever.
you have to
find
your people,
and then
you have to
let them
know
you're theirs.
and although
it's romantic
to try and
go it alone
you'll never
get anywhere
that way,
and I
happen
to know
you have
somewhere
you need
to be.

all the signs

hey,
that gun
to my head,
was that
you?
the one
that turned
and ended up
in my mouth,
was it
yours?
did you
have
anything to do
with that
rope
around
my neck?
I mean,
I don't want
to believe that,
it's just that
all the signs
are pointing
to you,
even if
you're just me
in disguise.
I'd like to
believe
otherwise
but
faith
has always
been…

topical

the specter of death
smiling,
Cleopatra
uncrossing her legs.
just a small glimpse
into the infinite
then it's over,
a bad dream
lingering
like egg yolk
or menstrual blood,
on your tongue.
I wonder what
the apostles
imagined
when they
masturbated?
I wonder
if they were
dreamt up guilty
and shameful
like everyone
else?

perhaps.

I wonder
if husbands
that stone
their wives
to death
hurl their stones
with secret
erections?

zealots
rolling their eyes
in the ecstasy

of prayer,
I wonder what
they see up there?

knowing starlight
is just as dead
as my mother's body
or my
father's soul.

perception
cursed by wisdom
is a heavy burden,
like love
to a prostitute
or epiphany
to a priest

but brutality
can never be
denied its beauty.
and innocence
is nothing
if not
made
to lose.

when the dogs howl
in the winter night
we assume it's the
cold,
we assume they
are suffering,
but what if it's
a primal
ecstasy we
subconsciously envy?

the specter of death
snickering,

a gym-coach
pedophile
ordering his boys
to shower.
the dark years,
the dark times
the dark eras
the dark and
the dark
and the dark

since time
immemorial,
since before
we could speak.
and it's still,
all we
talk about.

loud love
-for Luis C.

he promised me
a new bike,
and I promised
never to speak to him
in Spanish.
neither of us
knowing the other
any longer.
my first estrangement,
and here I thought
there would be only one.
so much time has passed
since that first cacophony
of slammed doors
and muffled screams,
and then he left

me crying
and *her*
bleeding

and for years after,
my mother
asking me:
do you have to
play it so loud?
do you have to
be so loud?

and this endless
ringing in my ears,
a constant reminder
that love, like hope
is loudest when it dies.

words of...

don't take your
loved ones
for granted,
they are not *required*
to love you.
never over eat,
there is nothing worse
than ruined pleasure.
what you think
you feel about sex
is just a thought
about a feeling.
death is
around the corner
live like you know that.
fear is a trap
like bravery is a hoax.
never trust your eyes
of all the senses
sight is the most
deceitful
your heart is a muscle...
exercise it / your mind
is an anchor
cut it loose.
your genitals are
an albatross,
don't swim
against the current.
cancers in your colon
are much like
humans in the forest.
giving pleasure
greatly increases
your ability
to receive it.
the word GOD
is only one syllable.

it should be two.
like HU-MAN
or MUR-DER
eat more meat,
it takes the edge
off your bloodlust.
don't shop so much,
it's depressing.
never criticize,
it only reveals
your insecurities.
good hygiene
is as courteous
as withholding
your opinions.
keep your nails clean,
you never know
when an orifice will
present itself.
live as free
as you can.
abstain from death
love with abandon
laugh heartily
sleep
as much
as you can
because
believe me,
one day
you won't
be
able
to.

dogma

stop,
please god
don't explain it
to me.
please don't try
to make me
understand.
listen…I know
it's important
to you
but seriously
all the more
reason
to just
leave it alone
you know
about alone.
you know

don't get started,
I know
you mean well
but fuck….no more
tonight.
it's been
a long day
and I'm dying.

inside joke

and what the fuck was I doing
in Chicago sleeping on the floor
next to my mother and her
stupid new boyfriend
except I wasn't sleeping
cause she wasn't sleeping
too busy sucking him off
under the cheap sheet
and I wasn't sleeping cause
the fucking sound of it
was so loud, all slobber
and suckle and this giggling
as grotesque as it was inexplicable
because how could it be funny
sucking dick on a floor
in cold ass Chicago next
to your god damn son you
never wanted
dragging a dirty blanket outside
to the 20 degrees I'd never felt before
a cold so sharp I thought my blood
would freeze but better there than in
with that awful laughter and the
shadow of my mother's head
bobbing under the pink sheet
and it was all just so fucking horrible
and I never could figure out
what the fuck was so funny

out there

tonight
she'll let you

and what if
the fairies
and the clowns
were theirs?
all this time:
there behind
the folds
of knowing

a knock
on the door
the phone
blinking
in the dark

get up baby
it's your mother
it's your father.

one good night's
sleep away
from OK.

Punk is dead
now
it's a dead scene

get to bed
you've got to
get up
early tomorrow
get out of
the murals
stay away from
that symbolic

language
you keep
mumbling
about.

it's a dead scene

no one goes
out like that
anymore

got anymore?

don't forget
you've got
laundry
tomorrow

I can't get
to sleep
there's
something
out
there.
you hear that?
͞

5

like a king

it was strange knowing my step-uncle had just fucked her. even though he used a condom I still imagined the stink of his dick on her pussy. the motel was dirty and I could see a wet washcloth crumpled on the bathroom floor. she told me to take off my pants and sit on the bed. I liked her telling me what to do. *your uncle tells me you've never been with a woman, is that true?* I looked down at her feet and mumbled *yeah, but he's not my uncle*....before I knew what was happening she stood in front of me and pulled down her panties. and there it was: my first pussy. it was hairy and I couldn't quite see her lips.... this disappointed me a bit...I really wanted to see it, I wanted to memorize it for future use but nevertheless, it was glorious. I breathed in the heavy animal odor...I thought about touching it....I wanted to get my fingers in there but then she got on her knees and to my surprise, there was a condom in her mouth, then with expert ease, she leaned into my crotch and slid it over my dick....with her lips, man...my first blow job.....I looked down to see if I could see it but the hair of her wig was covering everything. I did notice her ass though, it was big and white and I could feel my cock stiffen even more. I looked over to the mirror in the bathroom and I could just make out her ass and legs, it was fucking glorious....a half-naked whore, sucking on my sixteen year old dick, what a sight. after six or seven sucks she got up and leaned me back onto the bed, before I knew it she mounted me and slipped it in. it felt good in there. I wished I wasn't wearing a condom so I could feel more of her pussy...I tried to undo her shirt to get those titties out but she batted my hands away .....I felt scolded and let down....I always imagined my first time would involve sucking titties....it was the thing I was most looking forward to but then she put my hands on her ass. it was the first time I'd ever touched a naked woman's ass. I couldn't believe my luck....I really dug my fingers in there, squeezing those giant cheeks, pulling her ass apart and pushing it down further onto my crotch as she rhythmically rode me. I worried about coming too fast, I wanted the moment to last for a real long time, but then she leaned down and whispered something dirty in my ear, licking it a bit with her tongue... that was it....I couldn't take it anymore, I came in four or five epic explosions .I could feel her pussy muscles squeezing on my pulsing dick. I felt huge inside her....I felt like a man....like a king....and just like that...it was over. she hopped off me snapping the rubber off my dick on her way to the bathroom...I followed her with my eyes to get one last look at her big white ass.....it was nice...but then she squatted on the toilet and wiped her pussy with the wet washcloth from the floor....it was fucking disgusting. I wiped off with the sheet and quickly put my pants on...I really wanted to get out of there...I searched in my pockets to see if I had any money...I thought I was supposed to tip her or something....*don't worry baby, your uncle already paid*...she said from the bathroom and with that I was out the door mumbling some kind of *thanks, have a good night.* Have a good night? what an idiot thing to say. they say that you should try to make your first time special, that your virginity should be cherished and relinquished only to the gentle guiding light of love. but shit, sometimes you just get what you get, and I was alright with that.

tryouts

Julian:
man,
you gotta come over here!
I got a whore over here!
you gotta see this!
man, you can fuck her
if you want to!
seriously! she's gonna be
my whore!

I went over there,
sure enough
there was a naked white girl
on his bed.

Julian:
go fuck her man, she's ready!

so I did.
I went over there,
to fuck her.
she took me
into the bathroom
and leaned up
against the sink,
facing the mirror
and kind of
lifting her ass,
so I could
you know,
get in there.
I tried a few times,
but I just, couldn't
get it, in there.
I tried talking to her,
you know?
but she
wouldn't speak

that
fucked it up for me
somehow.

I pulled up my pants,
and got out of there.

Julian:
did you fuck her?
I told you man,
she's gonna be
my whore!
she's down to fuck man!

I just nodded,
and left.

first

you can
never
experience
something
for the
first time
twice.
like
smoking
crack,
or getting
a permanent
marker
shoved
up your ass
when you're
eight

these are
special memories
and no one
can take them
from you.
they are
yours
to keep,
cherish
them.

survival

sometimes you just
have to
lean into it
other times
you have to
lean back
and let it
come for you

sometimes
you have to
fight for it
other times
you have to
surrender,
and hope
for the best.

you can't
control it
all the time.
we're not
wired,
to drive it
all the
time.
sometimes
passenger
is best

I think about this
when I'm
starting
my car
or when
I'm taking
a shower
because

being alive
is confusing
and there's
really,
no one
right way
to do it.

as the suicides
mount
like bricks
in the walls
of cemeteries.

I think to
myself:
not everyone
survives,
not everyone
should.

dead, period.

remember that
poet,
that never
put
any periods
in his
poems,
because he
thought
that all
poetry
was
a vast
continuation
of all
that lives
in the
hearts of
men?
remember
him?
yeah?
me neither,
but I heard
he's dead
now.

ugly paintings

oh my dada Messiah
hissing
in violent mantra:
the end is dear!
the trap is fear!

gnarled fingers
of memory
pulsing,
a gash of meat
rotting the mind.
of your regret,
how much?
of your lives,
how many?
the lion smiling
behind
a muzzle of blood.
disaster
a choice,
as good as any.
how else to respond
or reciprocate
god's lurid gift?
a perspective slurred
and stumbling
toward oblivion.
prayers whispered
behind a wall
of apathy.

less and less mine,
less and less divine

needing trophies
for every scar,
twenty-two broken
teeth in a jar

a staunch futility
looming over
the time
that I
felt chosen
for something
greater,
the time
I believed
that life was
what you made it.

glaring into the
twitching eye
of the storm.
arrogant and swollen
with black blood
spilling
finally
a testament
to the
finality
of thinking.

one ordinary day
after the next,
conformity winning.
clarity
smearing this
limping,
wheezing
pretense

lost in the shadow
of a traitorous
memory
a peacock crawl
of shame and regret
from the bathroom
to the bed,

looking down at my
broken toes
my swollen knee
the scar of my
ancient,
3rd degree burn.
what was I supposed
to learn?

oh my dada whore
preening in front of
a hundred dirty mirrors
that hang
like ugly paintings
on the filthy walls
of imagining.

alone in a
small room
as the darkness
swallows everything
again

and the laughter
I hear outside
is mine
and the boy
crying
in the closet
is me

gratitude

I think my
father
is drinking
himself
to death.
he retired
back to the
homeland
and found
himself
a caretaker.
she's in her
thirties
and has
a fat ass
like he likes.
she fucks him
and feeds him
but he seldom
eats.
she keeps him
good and
drunk.
I see pictures
of him
on her social
media platform.
he always looks
lost and
haunted,
usually
with a shot
of Cuervo
in his
wrinkled hand.
I like
seeing him
like that.

when she's
in the pictures
she's always
smiling,
I like that
too.
she knows
that
I know,
what
she's doing,
just as she
knows
I didn't fly
three thousand
miles
last year
to stop him
but rather,
to see him off
and
thank her
for
her service

dying tree
- for Liz

alone
with the ancient words
stained into forever,
the sacred texts of men,
jettisoned across the aeons
revealing more and more mystery
beneath stars beneath science
and understanding, finally, fate's cruel
joke, the temptress knowing laying
eggs in the recesses of a thinking that
will not lay still, recesses where the light
cannot reach, where the words cannot
take root, a giving tree of taking grows
fed on shadows and endless doubts
an ever infinite *why* bellowed up
like an argument of noise pitched
to a cool silence that defies so much
more than time....
and this nagging, wheezing breath
insisting that I live and wonder
until it's over if it ever is.....
I close my eyes at night, trying
to silence the voices/thoughts
of the day/week/month/year
sometimes I picture your face
lips mouthing words to someone
like me that isn't me, but inevitably
you turn away, attention pulled
by some more tangible thing
something that exists in the real
we're calling real, in the real
that cannot be shared
where apples are eaten
and serpents are bedded
in the real where lives
are single, solitary things
with myriad players

in carnival costumes

I close my eyes at night
hoping, that one day
I'll awaken
and see whatever it is
I'm supposed to see
something to help me
become the you in me
I so desperately want
to be
and like the sun
I keep coming up
bright and
beautiful
and burning

envy

I empathize
with Satan,
I too,
know
what it's like
to fall out
of god's
good graces.
glowering beneath
unattainable
perfection,
alone
shining with
light, unseen.
a broken heart
bursting
with music
and envy.

but,
unlike Satan
the years
have
humbled
me
and
I've
made peace
with who
I am
and what
I have

finally
realizing
that god
is just
a broken

mirror,
slurring
back
my
perfect
form

finally
realizing
that
perhaps
god
should
envy
me.

the answer

love doesn't stop
the hate
in your eyes
from burning
gaping holes
into my heart,
love doesn't stop
my eyes either.

love doesn't keep
the obscenities from
flying out of your mouth
and into my tired ears,
love doesn't stop
my mouth either.

love doesn't
convince you that life
could never
have been better
without me
and if it does, you're
believing love's lies,
just like all the songs
said you would.

love doesn't follow me
when I run out the door
to get as far away
from you as I can
before I do
more damage
to an already limping romance
that might not survive
one more little insult.
love doesn't
keep you warm
when you're cold and

sleeping on the couch,
that's what rage
and regret are for.

love does not
cure boredom
love does not
stop redundancy
love does not
conquer all

love is not
the answer
because love
is not a question.
it's simply
all there is

**environ
mental
ist**

as much
a product
of our
environment
as wind
to ocean
or moon
to blood.
we flail
against
the relentless
gale of being,
like
sails
burning
above all
our best
intentions.

awareness is key

there are
things
around us
we can
never
change
but there
are other
things
we surely
can.

a little privacy, please

I need you to
promise me
you'll never
look in there.
I can't be around
all the time
so I'm just going to
have to trust you,
and you know that
doesn't comes easy
for me,
not even with you.
it's not that I don't
want you to see,
I'm just not sure
you'd understand.
and believe me,
that's no
reflection on you,
but there are
some things
you don't know
about me
dark and
complicated
things,
and if you
found them out
I'm not sure
I could explain
why they
aren't things
you should be
afraid of.

someday

I was
eight years old
the first time
I heard
a living thing
die.
I'd seen things
die, insects
mostly,
but I'd never
heard
anything die.

we had moved in
with my grandmother
and though I didn't
know this
at the time,
her house
was infested
with rats

then the time came
to bait the traps

I remember
watching my uncle
delicately placing
a chunk of
government cheese
on the little metal
plate
then carefully
pulling that
thick bar
against
the powerful spring
it all seemed

so dangerous
and fascinating
that's a huge trap,
I thought,
what the hell
kind of animal
are we trying
to catch?

I found out
early the next
morning

first I heard
the snap of
the metal bar
cracking on the
cheap wood,
followed by
a terrible shriek.
it sounded
like a baby
had been set
on fire
then I heard
my uncle laughing,
he was fucked up
but not enough
to get a kick
out of a burning
baby.
he went to
investigate
and within seconds
came back
with a
very large rat
still wriggling
in its trap
it's back

had broken
but it wasn't
dead yet.
he held it
upside down
hanging
by its tail.
it was thrashing
and screaming.
what a fucking sound.
I couldn't believe
my eyes.
its head was
shaking violently
from side to side,
it's eyes, wide and
scanning the room
much as I had done
when I first moved there

it wasn't
the worst thing
I had ever seen
but it was
definitely
different

I didn't like it.
I wanted it
to die already,
and it did
after a few more
very slow seconds.

and then
it was quiet

I didn't feel sorry
for it,
but I did

feel sorry
for myself.
I remember thinking:
why do I have to live
here?
why can't I
live with my dad?

I also
remember
thinking:
I'm
going to die
someday
and
I still
think
that.

how it goes
- for Cornell, for Bourdain

alone,
in a room
because it rarely
happens outside,
because it's
private,
until it's done,
then everyone
finds out.
I think about
them,
their final
thoughts,
their reasoning
if that can even
be applied.
are they calm?
sad?
completely
resigned?
or...
are there doubts?
maybe it's
free of thought
maybe it's just
an action
finally
unmarred
by so much
thinking
and as the life
begins
to slip away
I wonder
if they finally
feel some
relief?

some peace
even.
I don't know
it used to make
me so angry
like suicide
equaled
defeat
or cowardice
but time
has softened
this in me
now,
I just
sit with it
and think about
their
final moments
their eyes,
and what kind
of tears
might have
formed there
if any

wondering if
they were,
looking up,
or down,
or in.

patience

lying awake
at night
ten / twelve
fourteen years old
wondering how
I would do it
how I would
kill him
not just for me
but also
for the principle,
and although
it was not
about revenge,
I still felt a pull
to balance things,
a necessary
eradication
for which
I was obliged

sure
there was
hatred
but it was
bigger
than that
a vague
genetic
impulse
I didn't
need
to understand

hours spent
watching him
drinking coffee
cutting meat

licking grease
off his
fingers

I was fascinated

I pictured him
entering my mother
whispering
in her ear
telling her
how beautiful
she was
I pictured his face
the first time
he hit her,
the first time
he hit me

but it was
no longer
anger
that brought
these thoughts
to my mind
but rather
a calm
curiosity

the way
you watch
an alligator
in the zoo
hoping it will
move,
afraid that
it will

all my life
for as long

as I can remember
whenever I was
near him
there was always
something
that passed
between us
a simmering
resentment,
a secret
challenge,
as if I had been
the hammer
that nailed him
to his miserable
life
a hammer
he never saw
coming

watching him
aching for
reciprocation,
a valve
to finally
release
the hate he had
for both of us

I was aching
for it too

it would be
another
forty years
before
I finally
understood
why
I never did it,

why I stopped
wanting to.
I was just
too young
to understand

it was
never meant
for me to do,
life
would have to

I was just
impatient

but now
as the years
get closer
and we both
get older
I can just
ease into it,
relax and
wait
for the phone
to ring

neighbors

I see them
shuffling
in the alley
behind my
apart-ment
convening
in a constant
huddle of
boredom
and desperation
the stillness
of heroin
slowing every
movement
hushing their
voices
hours of nothing
but slow nods
and cigarette
embers
glowing
an occasional
word
exchanged
no laughter
no exuberance
just the slow
crawl of days
into weeks
months
into years
I watch
their dirty
fingers
scratching
at their
necks
when cars

drive by
they rarely
look up
sometimes
their heads
lift a bit
but never
high enough
to see more
than the
edge of the
asphalt
sometimes
they look down
at their hands
their dirty fingers
opening
and closing
into limp fists
and sometimes
I do this
with them
looking down
at my fingers
opening
and closing
but I never
make a fist

perhaps
I should.

intentions

I want to
love them
all of them,
pull their snouts
close to my lips
and kiss them
tenderly
run my soft hands
over their fur,
their scales,
their cancerous
skin
then stick
a few fingers in
I want to
take
their fear
from them
before it becomes
hatred
forgive them
for their
constant
humiliations
their
casual
degradations
I want to
celebrate
their
hypocritical
indiscretions
with my tongue
flicking
in and out
of their
artifice
I want to

love them
but I can't
because
I hate them
despite
all
my best
intentions
but I
won't
give up
on them
and
neither
should
you

significant *other*

there,
next to me
sitting too close
watching me,
whispering,
guiding,
insisting.

what are you
waiting for?
you know
you're going
to do it,
why not
do it now?

quick to
settle
an internal
argument.
practical,
if nothing
else.
his weight
on my back
his tongue
the slick
fork of it
licking
at my fear
his breath
so like mine
his voice
so like
father's.
I lift
an old cigarette
to my lips

that's it
and take a drag
wondering
which one of us
will die first
suspecting
but unable
to reconcile
that we're
one
in the
same

and this
distinction
joining
myriad
denials
I've mastered
avoiding

that's it
don't over
think it
just get it
over
with

and I do
and I
am

for the young

not so much
the suffering
itself
but more
the repetition
the constant
knowing
every reprieve
eventually
circles back

age does this
we become
cynical
difficult
to please
and slow
to rise

because
our bones
have been
through it
all before
and they're
tired

unlike
yours

understanding

transplanted
and cowering
in my
grandma's house
shocked by
all the casual
violence,
it occurred to me
that there were
no fathers
living there

none of my
uncles
even knew
their fathers
and now
I was like them
one of them

and the initiation
to this
terrible gang
was just
beginning

so I laughed
even though
I didn't really
understand

and these days
I laugh
because
I finally do.

murder her

I wanted to
hear you scream
it had been years
since I hated
someone
as much
as I hated
you.
I dreamt
of killing you,
with my
bare hands.
choking you out
until your
eyes went
gray.
watching
the shock
give way
to terror.
feeling your
body
struggle
beneath
the weight
of my
conviction,
your heels
kicking
at my shins.
I imagined
running my
hands
over the
bruises
and scratches
you would
leave

on my skin.
basking
in the sweet
aftermath
of your
just
demise
I thought
about it
so much
it began
to frighten me.
all the nights
you found
your way
into my
dreams.
your smug face
always
looking down
at me
the fucking
nerve
of you

now
in a way
I'm relieved
I got fired
from that
terrible
place
because
and even though
you're not
dead
you're
dead
to me
and that's

as close
to murder
as I ever
want
to get.

4

necessary consequence

I wake up in a strange room. The curtains are drawn and I can't tell what time it is, though I sense it's either very early, or very late. I realize I'm in a dingy motel and I wonder where I've left the drugs, probably on the table. I look for a table, but the room is
long and there's another room, just around a far wall. This frightens me. I know my mother is in that room. I get up off the bed and walk over, hoping to find nothing. I find myself walking down a long hallway I don't remember seeing. the closer I get to the next room, the brighter the light becomes. Soon it's burning my eyes and I consider turning back. I don't think I want to see what's in there anymore, but I keep walking, suddenly noticing I'm not wearing any shoes or pants. Finally I turn the corner and enter the brightly lit room. It's a hospital room. My mother is lying naked on what looks like an examination table. There are numerous electrodes and clamps fastened to her skin. She is screaming. Standing around her are five doctors wearing facemasks and holding clipboards. One of them motions for me to not come any closer. I begin to weep. *Don't worry*, one of them says to me, *the pain she is in, is a necessary consequence of her actions. All this is necessary.* I nod to signal I understand and keep a healthy distance. One of the doctors, the only female, lifts a slender looking cattle prod and begins to shock my mother. Her body bucks and writhes. She screams louder, her eyes locking with mine, pleading as if to say: *why are you letting them do this to me?* The pain I experience is visceral and immense. *This is not your pain,* says one of the doctors. *It would not be appropriate for you to take it from her, she has earned it and it is not yours to feel.* This comforts me and a warm indifference settles in. Suddenly I feel calmer than I've felt in years. I watch the doctors with a curious detachment. They really start to work her over. Cutting her with scalpels, pinching her with clamps, and shocking her with small white rods. Her screams begin to muffle and fade, as if sucked into a vacuum. This also comforts me. I decide it's time to make my way back to the table and find my drugs. I can't even remember what
kind I'm on exactly, but I suspect crystal meth. Sure enough, there's an open baggy on the table with two sloppily cut up lines lying next to a five dollar bill rolled up into a straw. The bill has had time to stretch and it looks ridiculously fat and comical. I can feel myself

smiling as I reach for it, wondering if I should tighten it or maybe just try to flair my nostrils big enough to accommodate its current size. I tighten it up and snort both rails, one in each nostril, and take a moment to drink in the miraculous burn. Holy fuck it hurts good. I consider praying and mumble something up into the light of the floor lamp. I find a smashed pack of cigarettes and fish one out, lighting it with some matches I find oddly familiar. Taking a long drag, I wonder if maybe my mom might want one, but then remember that she quit smoking several years ago….besides, she's got other shit going on. I figure I've got everything I need, just standing there, smoking, watching the smoke curl up in the air.

indication

the right arm
of the easy chair
stained and worn
the cushions
long since
surrendered
to the weight
of one collapse
after another.
deformed into
submission
and molded into
the contours
of waiting.

the rituals
of morning:
shower,
pull at my
foreskin
careful
to wash
beneath
the folds
that protect
me.
brush one
tired
tooth
at a time
dig at
last night's
meat
hiding
between them.
spit the
brown blood
down

the drain
my right arm
more tired
than my
left.
and I can't
remember
doing anything
with it
can't remember
much of
anything
at all

trapped together

a woman,
alone.
locked in
grief
behind a
locked door

weeping,
not quite
hysterical,
but close

her son
listening
from the
hall

is that
a fucking
Elvis
song?

and then
laughter
not quite
hysterical
but close

the
little boy
crying
in the
hallway

a woman
alone
a boy
alone

trapped
together

and no one
is coming

for either
of them

again

been blood

I warned you,
remember
the
daffodils?
the little girl
that was assaulted?
the one
no one
believed?

Hysteria,

I told you
this would
happen.

the night of
sudden
mescaline
the night
of too many
baggies
pulled
out of your purse

Curandera,

the nights
have been getting
strange

remember
the story
I told you
about that thing
that happened
when I was little?
I didn't tell you

all of it

te acuerdas?
the ghosts
have so many
stories
the dead
won't
lay still

a trumpet
calling the street
to attention

Tio, I remember
your sweet
Camaro
you tio?
you remember
that?
you remember
me?

Pandora

don't forget,
you carry
all of me
that's
left

vomit
glittering
on the sidewalk
something
that looked
like blood
something
that could have
been blood

making shapes,
symbols

a love letter
slanged
and pushing up
against
my eyelids

Tia, I'm sorry
I couldn't
follow you
to Christ

it's not
that I don't
believe
I just believe
in *more*

Papa
remember
when you
said:
a father
shouldn't have to
call his son.
what the fuck
was that?

the phone
on the table
a silent
accusation

papa,
I'm telling
you,
it wasn't
my fault

it was yours

above all else

if only you knew
that I learned
about Satan
from watching you.
that porno mag
you kept
underneath
your mattress,
I took a page out
and hid it
under mine.
titties on one side
and an
Aleister Crowley
article,
on the other.
jacking off
to the nipples
and reading
about the Beast
when I was done.
imagine the field day
my born again
Christian aunt
would have,
if she knew
that I learned
about Satan
from watching
you.
it made me wonder
just what kind
of shit
you were
really into.
knowing that sex
had something
to do with

why you abandoned
my mother and I
to go live
with that Tijuana
whore,
the one that let you
fuck however,
whenever,
and whomever
you wanted

so pardon me
for staring
at your dick
that one day
as you came out of
the shower,
I just wanted to know
what I had
to look
forward to.
I just wondered
what had led you
so far astray,
what was
so important
that you chose
impulse over
kindness,

and lust
above
all else

not quite love

for the longest time
she never let me
anywhere
near her clit.
it was like
she didn't trust me.
whenever
we fucked,
I got the feeling
that she was
using my dick
like a dildo,
guiding it
and straddling it
like only she
could determine
its purpose.
at first
I thought it was
hot,
but after
a few months
I began to wonder
why we couldn't
share
her pussy
together.
why she kept it
so
all to herself.
I didn't know then
about all the men
that had taken it
from her,
I didn't realize
how many years
she had fought
to get it back.

now, in retrospect
I guess I'm happy
I could help her
reclaim
what was
rightfully
hers.
I only wish
she had
given me
the chance
to show her
that I was
only
trying
to *give*
her
something,
not quite
love,
but
something.

backward four

after my mother
committed suicide,
(don't get it twisted
it wasn't some
dramatic
Hari Kari type
shit, just
pills, followed by
really sick after-swelling)
I got really curious about
how to make those
old cassette-style
four track recordings
because I had heard
that you could flip
the tapes and run
your tracks backward.
I can't tell you how much
that shit appealed to me
and wouldn't you know it, just
like that a fucking four track
just landed in my lap
I was so excited I didn't
even touch my guitar
for six months.
for six months
I just screamed
into a microphone
screamed
and spoke
and wept
and whispered
and ran everything
backward because
that was how
I was feeling
you wouldn't believe
how fucked up that sounded

the relief of
nailing down
the sound
of all those
terrible nightmares
these days
I still scream
but it's changed
now it's about victory
and survival
perhaps even
a little forgiveness
and maybe
that was the
point
you should
hear this
shit
it's fucking
ugly man
it's really
fucking
ugly
just like
me
then again
maybe you shouldn't
maybe no one
should
but still, I'm glad I did it
because I had to
and it's good to do
what has to be
done.

dis connect

on the morning
news:
a man was found
bleeding
in the front seat
of his SUV.
in the back seat,
were his three
dead sons,
ages: 8 /10 and 12
he apparently stabbed
his sons to death
and then stabbed himself,
but *he* survived.
I thought about him
laying in his
hospital bed
handcuffed to the rail.
I almost cried
but decided, instead
to distract myself by
looking at naked
women
on my phone.
then I
got aroused
and felt guilty.
so my mind
returned
to the wounded
father,
wondering
if *he* felt
guilty,
if he felt
anything
at all.
later

I drove to work
and turned my radio
to an NPR
station
and listened
to another story
about
Syrian families
drowning
in the ocean
bodies of children
washing up
on the beach,
then I cried.
penance paid,
I continued
driving
feeling better,
oddly calm
and subtly
human

pillar

the power
of all your
secret hurts,
the memories
you hide
under
dirty blankets
in your mind,
I can see that
sometimes
when you smile
and look down,
as if looking
for something
you might have
dropped.
I can see it in your eyes
when we make love
and sometimes
when we fuck.
if I could bury
my face
in all that hurt,
and lick at all those
tired wounds
that never heal,
perhaps I could
take some of it
from you.
but you'd have to
let me in there,
with no guarantee
that I wouldn't
make it
worse.

old man terror

we age
into our
terror
until
it becomes
a part
of us,
indiscernible
from our
very bones.
and
unless
we pay
careful
attention,
it's possible
to forget
it's there
at all.
this
is a
grave
mistake.
it is
important
to always
be aware
of it's
influence
over
the mundane
choices
we make.
for
in the end,
what are we

but a collection
of these?
the little
things
we did
or didn't
do
things
we should
have done
but chose
not to

because
we were
afraid,
and
didn't
know
that
we
were

free of you

my
little fingers
in your
big mouth,
your
ideas
shining
bad light
into my
gaping
head

I look up
at you
one last time
but I've grown
and you're
beneath me
now
so much
smaller
than I
remember

and this is
how
I want to
remember you
small and sad,
wondering
where
your stature
went

in that moment

a cluster of need
spilling blood into
the vast well of
of all my restless
thinking.
there amidst
the writhing ghosts
of long gone loves
that never
reciprocated
the desperate hope
I suffocated them
with.

me with my
head sewers,
ascribing death
and decay
to every
breathing moment.

a flood of fear
welling
in my chest
with a library of books
offering no solace,
only confirmation
that my terrors
are real
and necessary

and it's not death
I run from
in all those
terrible dreams,
it's not
the other side
that has me

weeping in one
used car
after another

I know I believe
in some form
that death
will be
a kind release,
but it's the act
of dying
that's worrisome.
knowing
in that moment
that you're leaving
everything
and everyone
you love,
everything
and everyone
that you've
ever *been*
in that moment
knowing
you're
never
coming back

older than me

like a body
purging
waste
in urine,
I wait
for nature
to rid me
of all my
worry
a process
older than me
sure to do
what needs
to be done.
dreaming
of disease,
a collection
of cells
dying.
the street
beneath
my feet
melting
and swallowing
me whole.
muted
screams
reaching
no one,
last words
choking
in my
throat.
out of reach
surviving
my shallow
breathing
a death hymn

of defeat
and surrender.

one day
my eyes
will open
to a world of no
remaining.
nothing familiar
no recognition
and I can't
imagine
anything worse.
a cacophony
of nothing.

and then
my eyes
will close
and never
open again,
and what
will I
see
then?

perhaps

It will
be
you
again.

never forget

smile because
you're dead.
smile because
you recognized
all the voices
in your head.
smile because
everyone
is suffering,
and it's good
to know
that it's
not just you.
smile because
you lost her
the moment
you met.
smile
because she's
a pain
you'll never
forget.
smile because
the parade
is for you,
and the song
of the marching band,
is yours.
smile because
your time
is through,
everything is done
and there's finally
nothing left
to do

paradox

my
you've
grown
into
quite
the fetching
paradox,
a strapping
failure
poised
for
success

are you
hungry?
here,
take
my
knife.

ours

when did we
deform,
become this
daily horror ?

with death
in our eyes
and someone
else's
blood
on our hands,
lost legs
stumbling
in the terrible
to and fro of our
meaningless lives.

work / TV / sleep /
weekend.
over and over
with carnage and
tragedy
all around us
encroaching upon
our minds
anaesthetized
to cruelty

perhaps
a kind of sleep
has done us in?
perhaps the
quiet lull
of rest
has closed our
eyes
and deadened
our hearts.

so much is
dangerous
to be open to,
toiling
beneath
the waves
of our souls
lost and frightened
consumed
by regret
and vapid
pre occupations

we used to be
so brave

wait

no we
didn't

bitter winter

I'm so close
to knowing
something,
I can feel it
in my bones.
but I don't
know what,
and worry,
I'll never
know.
I've wasted
years
worrying
about things
that never
come to pass.
like a bitter winter
I prepare for,
but never comes.
my fear like
unused jackets
hanging stiff
in the closet.
warm socks
and snow boots
I'll never wear.
in a way
it's like
preparing
for death,
because
when it finally
comes
what's there
to be ready for?

good night mom

I wanted
to ask you
about
your suicide
but it happened
so fast,
there wasn't
enough time
to ask you
why you did it.
there wasn't
enough
left of you
to question,
and you
didn't leave me
any answers.
no matter,
I'm sure you
had your reasons,
I just wish
I knew what
they were,
not that
that,
would have
made
any difference.
good night
mom,
I hope
you found
what you were
looking for.
I haven't.

hard earned bliss

far from the
prying eyes
of memory
I float,
like pollen
dancing
in the
ephemeral
wind,
guiltless
and without
shape.
I paid
good money
to get
here
I intend
to
stay
awhile.

space-base

I had met up
with my old friend
Shaon
to smoke
PCP.
I brought
ten bucks
to pitch in
on the pour
and gave it
to him
as I got into
his car.
after exchanging
the usual
pleasantries
we got down
to business.
aye bitch,
you ever tried
a space-base?
I didn't know
what that was
so he explained:
It's a primo
dipped in wack.

my curiosity
was piqued.
I had smoked
crack, PCP, and
weed before,
but never
simultaneously
of course
I said:
nah, let's do it!
how bad

could it be?
it was
pretty bad.
to this day
it's the worst
thing
I've ever
experienced.
let me tell you
about it.
it was a literal
trip to hell.
a rape of
consciousness
with no equal
and no comparison.
after the first hit
my mind and body
seemed to be
contorting
and arguing
with the very
laws of physics.
I heard terrible
sounds and felt
my flesh burning
and being ripped away
from my shattering
bones.
Shaon's face
twisted into
terrifying grimaces
and demonic shapes,
his voice rasping like
rusty iron rods
rubbing against
each other.
the world outside
was violently
shaking and I feared

the earth
would collapse.
I couldn't
remember who
I was or what
I had done.
couldn't figure out
what the creature
sitting next to me
was…but as it
leaned over and
passed me the joint
I hit it again. and
again. and again.
like a terrible
machine,
pre-programmed
to finish it.
I was sure
I was going to die.
after a time,
I welcomed it.
anything to make
the horror of it
stop.
somehow, I managed
to drive myself home
and spent hours
listening to the secret
gears in my walls
turn and grind.
the last thing I remember
was promising god:
if I survive this night,
I will never
ever,
smoke
the *space-base*
again.
a promise

I kept.

in retrospect,
I'm still glad
I tried it

3

i did that

I had spent most of the night making out with this metal head chick Julian had introduced me to. I didn't really know her but she was really into kissing me. well, really into kissing anyway.

she was so horny and kept grinding her legs into my groin. we made out for hours underneath the bridge of the L.A. riverbed. after a while, it got late and it was time to go. I had nowhere to take her, so I headed back home. Alone. I was living with my mother and her brother and their spouses. really no place to bring a horny metal chick. after so many hours with a terrible erection my balls were hurting something awful. it was late and I was pretty drunk but decided to cruise down main street anyway, to check out the downtown whores. the scene was jumping. it must have been near three in the morning but the sidewalk was crawling with whores. I wasn't the only horny guy out there either. there were dozens of cars, driving slow and pulling up to the curbs. I spotted this big girl with giant tits that she shook and squeezed with her hands. I pulled over a few cars up but I was too slow and caught sight of her in my rearview hopping into some other guy's car. I pulled away and was nearing the end of the strip and getting ready to go around the block for another pass when I saw her: a beautiful, young chola, standing all by herself. at first, I thought she might not be a streetwalker at all, maybe just high and trying to score a ride. but then she looked at me and forced a smile so I pulled over and she got in without saying a word. it was strange. we sat there in silence for a few seconds as I stole glances at her body and her face. I couldn't believe my luck. she was so pretty, with an amazing set of tits and big full lips I knew I'd never kiss. *take a right at the next street up* she said, so I did. we parked behind a dumpster a few blocks down. then she looked at me and said: *50 bucks.* I nodded and pulled out my money. I didn't have any change and wondered if I should ask her if she had any but that seemed crude, so...*I gave her sixty.* soon she was wriggling out of her jeans. but she didn't take off her shirt. that bummed me out a little, I really wanted to see those tits. I had a pickup truck and soon she was stretching out on my bench seat. I opened my door and got out so I could drop my pants. that's when I saw it. her beautiful little pussy. dressed in this downy patch of hair. again, I couldn't believe

121

my luck. she didn't even seem like a whore…it was nice, I thought…I could pretend that I somehow managed to get a pretty girl from the neighborhood to fall for me. I was immediately hard and climbed up on top of her. as I slipped it in it occurred to me that I didn't have a rubber on and was curious why she didn't ask for one. this bothered me a little, but I was drunk and to be honest it kind of excited me. her pussy was like a dream, so small and tight. I was in heaven. after a few strokes, I looked down at her eyes. I wanted to see her pretty face, the face I had paid *sixty dollars* to look at, but she had her head turned away and her eyes were closed. there was this terrible sadness on her face and that's when I noticed, how young she was. she couldn't have been much older than twenty. I don't know why this bothered me, but it did. I tried to focus on her lips and the feel of her pussy on my dick…and just kept pumping away at her, suddenly wanting it to be over already. then I was struck by this terrible odor, coming up from our sex….it was bad…like old fish and drying semen. I wondered how many other guys had already fucked her that night? I wondered what she was using to wipe off with? it was very distracting. I worried I might lose my erection, so I opened my eyes to get a look at her pretty face, hoping to get the smell and the images of other men out of my head…that's when I noticed she was crying. this lonely streak of tears, was just rolling down her pretty face. it was the saddest thing I had ever seen, and it was happening because of me. I wanted to jump off of her and apologize but before I could stop what was happening, I came. she furrowed her eyebrows and a few more tears squeezed out of her tightly shut eyes. I felt like the biggest piece of shit that had ever walked the earth. I climbed off of her and wiped off with my shirt, pulling my pants and boxers up with one quick motion. by the time I got back in the truck, she was dressed and sitting very straight, looking out the window. I knew I had made a terrible mistake. I knew the night would haunt me for the rest of my life, (it did) *take me back to main street* she said, so I did that.

Crow

I slip into
bed with it
quietly,
not wanting
to wake it,
not wanting it
to know
how late it is,
it stirs as
I slip
my cold feet
under
the blankets,
and I lie there
motionless,
waiting
for it's
breathing
to slow
and deepen.
then,
when I'm sure
it's sleeping
soundly
I turn
toward it
hoping to
dream
of flying
again.

careful
not to crush
its wings.

insight out (god within)

a prescient
weight
a stone
atop a vein
pressure
more than
thinking
the vulgar
words
cowering
beneath
intent

meaning
all around
floundering

measuring
nature's bad
call, a whisper
to disease
festering
over sex

looking into
a black mirror
shining,
the history
of alchemy
smiling
I move
toward it
nature
spreading
her legs
Pleroma
glistening
in the after light

of Gnosis

the terrible
aftermath
of a dated
faith

consciousness
more
than a stream
tendency
more
than it seems
as light
gives way
to dark
again.

noise

one singular
moment
after another,
the compilation
of which
a foundation
can be
built upon,
if we dare
to question
the sedative
explanations
we've been
programmed
to believe.

the schizo
phrenic
frag
mentation
of all
our
embittered
selves is
by
de   sign,
a blanket of
inertia
provided to erase
the notion
that
our inherent
grace
has been
disguised
as sickness.
because comfort
and hedonism

feed apathy
and complacency
be cause
en lighten ment
threatens
darkness,
but
what if we emerge?
guided by
the pale
flickering
of our de-valued
intuitions.
learn from our
shadow selves
negate
consume and forget:
the mantra
we've been fed

what if we
raise
our silent voices
and
disrupt
the quiet
that is
expected
of us
with noise
noise
noise

grief

I don't visit
the cemetery much.
maybe I should
but I find it hard
to sit there
on that strange hill.
it always
brings me back
to the day
of the funeral.
I don't want to have
anything more
to do
with that day.
It's not what I want
to remember
when I think
about her.
come to think of it,
I haven't really
decided
what it is
I DO
want to remember
about her.
I guess
that's the problem,
and going to the
fucking cemetery
isn't going to
solve it.

where?

down the barrel
or the ladder,
near the eye
and beneath
my father's belt.
found there
among the ruins,
spotted two miles
west of the
accident site.
an open
invitation
lying, face down
amidst
a clutter of
coupons
panties
on the floor,
bra
hanging
next to a
moldy towel
in the bathroom.
in the eye
of a dirty needle
a blood stain
on the cleaver,
chicken parts,
burning
in the freezer.
there,
right there.

think positive

the speakers crackle and hiss,
a distant reminder that
time and space have more
corroborators
than I do.
it doesn't matter
if death is a trick,
only whether or not
I fall for it.
waiting for the music to do
what it's supposed to,
but this, like all my expectations,
falters beneath
the weight
of my incessant
need.
I'm so tired.
tired of waiting for something
to happen
tired of wanting to be kinder
or more considerate
than I am.
what's the matter with me?
I'm coming apart.
I know that now.
I would say:
it's just a matter of time,
but of all the clichés,
I hate that one
the most.
wondering why I asked
the dark to carve a moth
into my leg,
why I insisted
on corpse green wings
and pretty eyes,
why I insisted

that the skull
be prominent
and full of grace

waiting for the music
to do what it's supposed to,
but it doesn't work for me
or answer to anybody.
I want to be like the music.
I'm tired of
answering to so many,
their legion mouths
flooding my ears

what's the matter?
what's up with you lately?
you need to snap out of it.
stop focusing on the negative,
you have to think positive.
do something constructive.
go out there and be active!
get some sun.

stop it

don't over-think it,
that's a trap.
keep moving,
if you slow down,
it gets
it's claws into you.
you won't feel it
at first,
no one does.
but as sure
as the sun rises,
it will begin
to drag you down
and soon
it will get harder
for you to move,
harder
to get up,
and eventually
it will make you
still.
and just because
it happens
to everybody
doesn't mean
you should let it
happen
to you.

wide open

I don't have a
dodger game
to watch
or a fantasy
football team
to monitor.
not paying for
the big fight
and
there aren't any
'boys'
for *boys night out.*
no tittie bars,
no side piece
to fuck at lunch.
I don't work on my car
or toss the football
with my son.

I don't even cheat
on my wife.

tomorrow
I'll take my son
to a matinee,
something disturbing,
to fuck
with his head.
next month
I'll push him
into his first
slam pit.

raising him
the only way
I know how,
with my heart
and mind

wide open.
hoping one day
he'll look back
and think:
my dad was
alright
he was
kind of
a trip.

the secret

waiting for the bus
for the train,
waiting for the
hour-hand
of the clock
to catch up
with the minutes

waiting for death
for rebirth,
for a moment
to just breathe
like they do
in yoga,
real slow
and with
nothing else
on your mind.
I try to calm
down, try
to get to a
quiet place
without
want,
without
desire.
a moment
without
waiting.

but I can't

a twitching
nervousness
keeps stirring
the worms
in my center
I don't know

what the secret is,
but I know
it has something
to do
with love
and the end
of fear,
knowing
to be truly
free
I must get
to a place
where I'm
no longer
waiting
for anything

but it
hasn't
happened
yet

and
I'm getting
tired
of waiting
for that
shit.

time of our lives

what a
wonderful
tragedy
we were,
dancing
in the sunshine.
stupid,
high,
at one
with the
chaos
we worshipped

the death
about us
is what I miss
most.
the sweet
fuck
of danger

we were
so beautiful,
shiny
and basking
in the glow
of abandon.
making
hopelessness
seem
elegant
and
cavalier.

nostalgic for
the glory
of our
surrendering

to the risk
of everything.

I really
was
having
the time
of my life,
and so
were you,
weren't
you?

your face

not your
fucking face
again.
not today,
not *again*.
I've gone
so
out of
my way
to express
just how
much
distaste
I have
for your
face and
I have gone
to great lengths
to keep
mine
to myself.
so please
if you could
just
keep *yours*
away.
Please.
I really
don't want
to have to
ask you
again.

$4.89

half way through
a very expensive
cup of artisanal
coffee, I was struck
by a sudden need
to relieve myself
as I entered the
coffee parlor's
predictably pristine
restroom
I was assaulted
by a powerful
aroma that
can only be
described as
a thick
brown fog
of rancid
animal waste
the stink
was so palpable
I felt
confronted
by it
you can
guess my
concern:
microscopic
fecal
particulates.
understand
I'm no miser
but I was
not about
to leave my
coffee
unattended
in a crowded

coffee parlor
and risk
some well
meaning
barista
throwing it
away,
so, of course,
I took it,
in there,
with me.
after relieving
myself
I washed my hands
and left
but could not
escape the feeling
that I had
brought something
out with me.
and now
It was surely
in or around
my cup
of coffee
don't get me
wrong,
I kept
right on
drinking it
but it was
not the same.
though I couldn't
taste any difference
my mind
had already decided
there was.
after every sip
I kept looking down
at the cup

studying
the little brown
drops on the rim
feeling the warmth
of it
in my hand
when I was done
I threw the cup
in the trash
and thought about
what had
happened,
what I could
have done
differently
how I could have
affected
the outcome.
I thought about
the man
that had caused
that malodorous
catastrophe
what he could've
eaten that would
generate such
an apocalyptic
aftermath
considering
my position
as a wartime
journalist
of the human
condition
I pondered
the existential
lessons
of my experience
but, like many
of the great

philosophers
I was left
with more
questions
than answers

and with that
I went back to
work
and wrote this
in the hopes
that some day
a person might
read it
and offer
an answer
to the world
something
the people
can use
to guide them
to help
them
in a way
that I
could
not

the waiting

what? you thought
you'd be spared?
missed, somehow?
maybe you
thought
you were so good,
nothing bad,
would ever
happen to you.
not me
I knew I had it
coming
just as I knew
it was always
coming *soon*.
I remember
when I was young,
time after time,
thinking: is this it?
is this the big
bad thing
that's supposed
to happen to me?
every time,
I was wrong.
something worse
always came.
now, I don't
sit around
and wait for it
anymore.
finally understanding
that the big
bad thing
is the waiting.

post-genesis

the lines are drawn
long before
we are born,
centuries of
twisted sheets
and grunted
couplings.
we are but
the outcome
of semi sentient
co-conspirators
that never
considered
their flawed
legacy,
its generations
of influence
or the lineage
of its pain;
and what
we take and bestow
from the cradle
to the grave
is ultimately
what
defines us.
who we are,
building
and growing,
all the while
our minds,
fussing over
everything,
and
everyone else.

prism

there is a reason
that blood is red,
or I should say,
there is a reason
that red is,
what red,
has always been:
a cause for alarm.
perhaps the first
color we see,
the blood of the womb
pushing up against
an unwelcome sun,
and the coming of
the spectrum
of our lives.
yes, there
in this prism
of eternal affectation,
our precious lifetimes,
lit for just
a moment,
by a light
we try,
but cannot
understand.
there is a reason
dark is said
to be imperceptible,
another
clever illusion
conjured up
by men with
more than light
to obscure.

pedestal grave

a sharp knife
for the serious
cutting
an elegant pen
for the
grace incision

your eyes
smiling at
my slut face,
beautiful.

looking back at
a pure self
revealed.
atrophied
and scarred
a rat's
embryo
floating
in a jar

understand that
it's you
because
you laid
your eyes
on me

when you
should have
looked away

I understand
you don't
see things
my way
but you

should
understand
there isn't
another,
not for you,
not tonight.

.

kindness

I know I've gone
too far
I can feel it
in my bones
and in the way
she looked at me
when I started
screaming.
when did being right
become so important?
I think of all
the things
I've trampled,
stomping away
in some grand gesture
of righteousness
or finality.
as if my exit
could ever
signify anything
other than
cowardice.
me and my
big ideas.
I'll show them,
I'll show her.
one slammed door
after another.
where is the
gentleness
I seek?
why do I cower
away from it?
reaching
in the dark
for a kindness
I've had to
learn

exists
reaching
because
I don't
want to lose
anyone
else

resonance

you don't always
remember
the details.
what day
of the week,
what year,
how old you were
exactly,
but you remember
the flush of heat
on your face.
you remember
the fear,
humiliation,
panic,
the inevitable
rage.
it's curious what
stays with you
and what
fades.
it's curious
how trauma
and violence
always
resonate
louder
than
tenderness
or
love.
perhaps
that's why
he hit me
so hard.

bad Spanish

a whirlpool
of wanting
pitted against a
sea of knowing.
how were we
ever expected
to transcend
an infinite
we could
never
comprehend?
lost from
the start,
two
backward arrows,
flung
into
our
bleeding hearts.
one part regret,
two parts fear
and the bible
just bad Spanish
that didn't
hand down
as sacred,
as intended.

drag

the word is dead,
or so I've heard.
no light
anywhere,
no hope in sight.
the earth?
she's fucked too.
and if she is
then so are we.
right?
oh but the
Christians
are having
a field day!
finally,
the prophecy
is fulfilled!
The End of Days
is upon us!

the problem
with not believing
blindly,
and questioning
everything,
is that you never
truly get to know
anything
for certain,
except for
maybe,
the nature of
your *self.*
and that's
a colossal drag.

**god is looking up into an unforgiving
sky and finding a smile, curling, at the
corners of your lips**

two broken umbrellas,
propped against the base
of a podium I bought to
help me with my
demonic sermons.
a chipped ashtray
resting on the piano
I don't play because
because I can't afford
to tune the evil keys
properly
five memories,
I've been running from
all my life
two car keys,
for cars I don't
own anymore
two un-played guitars
gathering dust in the closet
because they
don't sound right
because I
don't sound right
38 pills in the cabinet
27 beers in the fridge
a picture
of my dead mother
in an old wallet
I don't use.
I know what I have.
I know what I am.

lesser man

as animals,
and as
prone as we are
to folly,
it should
come as
no surprise
how often
we fall
just short
of grace.
ultimately
we are reduced
to the idle
contemplations
and accomplishments
we've accepted
as meaningful.
and who dares
question
in this day
and age,
something
as outdated
and old fashioned
as the
state
of one's
soul?
just me,
and maybe
you

word

there is no
scarcity of
sacred texts,
my book
shelves
are stuffed
with them.
does it matter
that I prefer
the book
of Baldwin
to the book
of Luke
or Job?
that I
trust
and value
Carver
over
Christ?
isn't it
ultimately
a matter
of
personal
taste?
that your
piety
compels
you
to take
to the
street corner
with
bullhorn
and sign
is not
for me

to judge,
that your
orthodoxy
prohibits
consorting
with
some of
the more
salacious
genres
is not
for me
to question.

my only
critique
is one of
variety,
no matter
how enamored
you are
with it's
verses
and prose,
how can you
not
grow tired
of reading
the same
god damn
book
over
and over
again?

consolation

more of it's
mouths
whispering
in my ear,
more of it's
ideas
manifesting
as mine.

less
resolve
less
will.
less and
less
and less.

understand,
it says,
there is no
winning.
only
different
takes
on the same
defeat

less
resistance

more
and more

surrender

cubensis

my ear,
falling off
there on my lap
looking at me
asking me for help
this little
silent, ear
talking to me
telepathic shapes
undulating out of it
in waves
geometric
glowing
there on my lap
transmitting
multi-frequency
inter-dimensional
you know…
you know dimensions,
and these tiny
letters I'm
typing, just
sinking
further and
further into
this screen
that just
keeps getting
deeper and deeper
and why is it orange
when it used to be
white?
suddenly so many
different kinds of light
and some of it is thick
like a translucent fog
a glowing mist
that isn't wet

though I can't
remember what
wet is
exactly
suspecting there
might be more
to it than water
my little ear
murmuring
something
into my leg
and I could
feel its heartbeat
as the screen
gets deep into
this growing
cone that
spirals down
into an infinite
light too beautiful
to articulate
the stupid words
flashing their
teeth
the light getting
brighter as it gets
further away
which brings it
closer somehow
spilling
geometric insight
of the vegetable mind
super-imposing
over mine
an epic collapse
of rationale
like a heavy semen
exploding into color
physio-astro-gnostical
multi-positional

awareness
old thinking limping
out into the hall
leaning all angles
and bad geometry
and then
hundreds of elves
convening on
a terrace in my head
thick columns
shining, black
and impossible
marble
divine architecture
shifting mass

my little ear
down there
in my lap
swelling,
color striking
the cortex in
thought prism
a spiritual
synethstesia
inverting this
flesh-like
perspective slang
that is just so
god damned
funny
the cosmic giggle
echoing back
into the mystical
reaches of
alchemical
time
ancient sorcerers
smiling up
from beneath

the heavens
as above so below
jelling,
manifesting
a woman made
of clouds
and rain
getting wet
though I cant
remember
what wet is
exactly
suspecting it might
be about
something
more than water
there, in my head
my little ear
saying something about
a sentient spectrum
a collective consciousness
transcending matter
feelings
plus odors times
minutes cubed
the dolphin mind
the eagle's eyes
the fourth dimensional
world of the wolf
a scream down an
alley of broken science
the stench of cages
explanations / categorizations
theories disguised
philosophies in drag

bright chaos
- perfect
- astonishing
there

to the brink
of madness
and beyond

it's so funny!
so absurd!
I get it now!
all this time
I thought
oh man,
my sweet
little ear!
thank you!
my sweet
listener,
for helping me
see finally
with my
heart and
not my head

with my soul
no longer
dead.

2

still waiting

I could see the outline of her naked body beneath her thinning night dress. *come on, it's time for you to take your bath. you're fucking filthy. c'mon, get in there.* she shoved me into the bathroom and I could hear the lock in the door, click behind me. shit. I was locked in. so I took a bath. a long one. I dried off, put on the pajamas I had been wearing, and knocked on the door. *okay mom, I'm done with my bath.* nothing. *I'm clean now mom!* nothing. I sat down and waited for what seemed like hours. I put my ear to the door and listened for any sounds. I could hear my mother crying and talking to somebody. shit, she's on the phone, I'm gonna be here all day. after a while I could tell she wasn't on the phone, she wouldn't say the shit she was saying to anyone on the phone. she was talking about my father and sounded a bit hysterical. I got bored and started digging in the little cabinet under the sink. there was all kinds of shit in there. all these cleaning products and one very menacing looking spray bottle. it was tall and had this vicious red nozzle. that's it, I thought. I'll make a murder spray. I had used RAID before and marveled that a death spray existed and people could use it to make shit die. I wanted to make shit die too. I could start with the roaches and move my way up to bigger things. I began by pouring a bit of each chemical under the sink into the spray bottle, the combination of which, I was sure, would be deadly. after the poison was mixed and loaded, I waited patiently for some living thing, to come crawling out. some shit to kill. something that needed to die. my eyes scanning all the cracks in the floor. waiting, as my mother wept and muttered, from the other, side, of the door. I waited for a long fucking time, but the only thing I wanted to kill, was on the other side of the door. Eventually, my mom let me out. I spent hours relishing in the thought that I had a secret bottle of murder spray hidden under the sink. I knew one day, I would get the chance to use it. There were so many things I wanted to kill. so much shit that had to die. I couldn't wait. I suppose, in many ways, I'm still waiting in that bathroom for something living to come crawling out. waiting for something big to kill.

gnosis lurking

approaching,
cautious

faith
fermenting,
souring

holy canon
leaning
toxic

an inner
crouching

something
vital
to apprehend

something
needing
its own
death

investigating
multiple
outcomes,
infinite
scenarios,
and
parallel
positions
behind
the veil

and there
just behind
the soft
periphery

Hermes
laughing
beneath
the seems

finding myself
suddenly
laughing
too

for now,
I understand
if only
just
for now.

hereditary

sometimes,
I dream
in Spanish.
it's the strangest
thing.
I don't know
why it happens
or where
it comes from.
I figure
it must be
in my blood.
genetic memory
and all that.
like when I eat
plantains
or black beans.
there's this
odd feeling
that I'm supposed to be
remembering something.
but I don't know what.
at times
like these,
I think about
calling my father
in Costa Rica,
but I know how that
will end,
and always
decide against it.
sometimes
I wish I could
call my mother,
but she's been dead
for nineteen years.
sometimes
I think about

calling her anyway,
her old number
swimming
somewhere
in the back
of my mind.

sometimes
I dream in Spanish,
knowing full well
there's no one
in my family
left alive
to do that with.

maybe
it's
hereditary?

maybe it's
nothing.

c'mon, c'mon

It is always
the last few
minutes
that destroy us.
the last few
moments,
that are
truly
unbearable.
never mind
of what.
it could be
of love
of life
of joy
even of pain.
it is always
the last few
that do us in.
it is those
we cannot
survive.

so in an effort
to persevere,

I propose

that every
thing
and every
one
just get on
with it
already.

hopes and dreams

I was in the 7th grade
at my first
junior high school
dance.
standing against
the wall, I was
trying to work up
the courage
to ask a girl
to dance with me.
I was a rocker
so the disco
that was playing
did not appeal
to me,
but I wanted
to kiss a girl
and I figured
dancing with one
was a good
first step.
after forty minutes
of nervously
standing around,
I spotted the most
beautiful girl
and walked
right up to her
and asked:
would you
like to dance?
I was terrified.
she looked at me
and then looked
around the place
and said:
with *you?*
then she laughed

and walked
away.
humiliated
and hurt,
I walked
back to the wall.
why did she
have to laugh?
I didn't ask
another girl
to dance
until I was
23 years old.

I often think
of that day
and wonder:
whatever happened
to that girl?
and although
I know it's petty
I always hope
and dream
that she
died alone
of rectal cancer
in a dimly lit
hospital room
with brown
blood
dribbling
out of her
rotting
ass.

affinity

though you couldn't
see them,
I knew there were heads
mounted on the wall,
a collection of dead
all secretly hanging
plain as day
if only you could see them
like I could
and perhaps
that's why I was there,
to witness
the invisible carnage
displayed so prominently
for only me
to see.
it has always been
this way,
monsters have always
had a tendency
to reveal themselves
to me,
as if my
frequency
beckoned
revelation.
I suppose
I could blame
a certain
affinity,
but it is not
admiration
that holds
my attention
but rather
a deep need
to understand
the nature

of the beast
that sleeps
within us all.
in an effort
to identify
and recognize
the signs.
how else
can I hope
to avoid
becoming
one of them,
or at least
recognize
if I already
have?

taming

my trying
to bring it
down
to paper
an origami
of folding
word

wanting
more than
a simple
harnessing,

the wanting:
a soft cage
to waste a life in

the things
I make
holy
faltering

paying the price
of language
the fucking
humiliation,
ornate
stories
that didn't
age well

what have we
been saying?
a droll
legacy
stammering
from the past
to the omnipresent

now

why
in-sight
not out?

the mystery
of letters
decided
by the
dead
again

the fear
to join them
another cage
whose bars
I polish
with denial

my heart
locked
within
the
confines
of inherited
words

feeling my
way out

following
a path
of poems

poser
- for Tom Araya

after my mother killed herself
I found myself, more and more,
in the slam-pit w/ my uncle Pablo,
getting the shit kicked out of us and
kicking the shit out of all our grief.
turning all that dark into fuel for the
fire already burning inside us,
so many shows I lost count.
sometimes bands I didn't even like:
cannibal corpse or lamb of god
deicide and death angel
then one night we went to see
SLAYER in fucking Orange County.
it was brutal. five minutes in
and one of my eyes was already
swelling. there was so much blood
and so many neo Nazis , I actually
began to worry a bit. but then
something strange happened:
suddenly Tom Araya, stopped playing
mid-song and went into a speech.
something about his father's
recent death, and his new-found
realization that there was more
to life than violence, and destruction,
more out there than blood and Satan.
and he asked that we consider
an end to our blood lust and fury.
and everyone booed. and he got angry
and I thought: Tom, you started fucking
SLAYER. you've had 25 years to put
some kindness or humanity in your music.
25 years to realize your band was just
a one trick pony. but you did nothing.
you made one album after another
all the same and all interchangeable
SHOW NO MERCY

SOUTH OF HEAVEN
HELL AWAITS
GOD HATES US ALL
and on and on
and now your father died
and your heart is breaking and you
can't understand why
people are so violent?
well Tom, the thing is,
all people *aren't* so violent,
but people that listen to *SLAYER* can be.
and why do you think that is Tom?
Fuck you Tom Araya, you fucking poser.
I suppose, since my mother killed herself
I should start writing delicately worded prose
about hope/love/god and the gentle light at the end
of the fucking tunnel. should I do that Tom?
I suppose that we should all wait around
for a nice and pertinent death
to wake us from our sleep?
all these years and you never once
thought about the redundancy
of your message or the
singularity of your intent?
now you want your fans to change?
If I wanted a fucking speech
I would have gone to see
Rage Against the Machine.
Fuck you Tom Araya,
you should have thought about that shit
a long fucking time ago.
enjoy your fucking skin heads.
next time, I'll go see
CONVERGE instead.

argument with self

you,
beaten,
abandoned
crawling across the
waste of
all you might
have been.
lost,
dead,
less than alive

get up

you,
with your stitches curling
into ugly scars,
with your eyes
blinking at an
unforgiving sun.
flames licking
at the heels
of all
you chose
to forget.
get up, break free
you have become
a fly flailing
in a spider's web.
your death throes
echoing down
corridors of regret.
drinking in rooms
where you hide secrets
too painful to confront,
afraid of everything
you refused to see
tangled up in myth
and clamoring

for belief
belief in something
belief in someone
other than your own
fractured selves.
a moth circling
a self-made
flame,

and if
there is
something
to be gained
from
reconciliation,
I'll
never know
because
we
no longer
speak

you're welcome

the particulars
are not important
all you need
to know is
she died
kicking and
screaming.
what you
need to know
is that,
if her
fingernails were
ever found,
my skin and blood
would be
underneath them

these are
the details
that should
concern you,
these
and that you
smiled

when you
heard
she was
dead,

and that
you
didn't
have to
do it

running low

two more left,
two cigarettes
two beers
two hours,
before
the liquor
stores close

I've got
two good years
and then
I don't know

two lines,
at least
three more
hours to go.
what do I do
now?

one
decision
left to
make

it's
getting late
running low
twenty
dollars left
just enough
time
to get a little
closer
to death

awake

an emission
that stained
the fabric
between
worlds

a stain
that'll never
come out

ideas
forming,
nebulous,
without
intent,
without
purpose

then something
like a curtain
parting

there
where the
burden lifts

a carnival
archetype
leering
all
red paint
and
scary eyes

and when
the river
rushes
and the

alligator
rears its head,
it's bigger
than I
remember,
bigger
than I
imagined

and I wake up
sweating
and I
almost
remember
why
this time,
but it
fades

I fade

arrival

a soft
meat
dripping
with life

a sharp knife

quiet

emerging
from
behind
the din.

the roar
finally
receding

but the
quiet
brings
no comfort
just more
silence
to fill

with
screams

words fail

did you feel that?
what was that?
did you dream
a river too?
what is that?
how could..
why does…
did you feel that?
what IS that?

I'm sorry,
you're tired,
no
I just meant,
I didn't mean
to imply
wait..
you're not
tired?
then what…
why did I…
OK, I see
no, I get
what you mean
isn't it
a trip though?
when it gets…
the way
it's been
getting…
when we…
the thing
where
you…
I know,
you're right,
in a way
it's almost

impossible
to talk about

yeah,
I'm getting
tired too.
let's go
back to bed
I'll hit
the lights

telling

a bruise
spreading,
changing
color

quiet,
before
the police
come

smiling
in the mirror
the holes
where teeth
used to sit

black men
gathering
in a white
neighborhood

vultures
circling
high
in the sky

something
dead
down here

somewhere
a baseball game
playing
on a radio

polio trees
doing nothing
but standing

their roots
suffocating
beneath the
asphalt

the night knows
something
it isn't telling

father and son
clenching
teeth
beneath
a beat up car
cancer ritual
dripping oil

here come
the men in
white coats

an ambulance stalls,
sirens blaring

'as good
a night as any
to die.'
she says.
then does

the night
knows something
I've always
known

.

1

getting inside

at one time, it had been, just the garage, but now it was my uncle Ismael's room. he kept it locked with a giant padlock, which of course, just made the rest of us that much more curious about it. it only took a couple of weeks before my uncle Pablo had managed to get his hands on a key. and after a few days, he finally let me have a peek inside. there was one wall completely covered in porno magazine centerfolds. I couldn't believe my eyes. it was glorious. I was only seven, so Pablo thought my amazement was hilarious. *bitch, whatchu know about pussy?* I was embarrassed but felt like I had some kind of understanding about how powerful those images were. they stirred something inside of me. something big and strong, which I found immensely alluring. it was good to feel something big and strong. I marveled at how many of the women were holding their pussy lips open with their fingers. I concluded that that was something that nasty women did; hold their pussies open with their fingers. there was something about the way they looked into the camera. it was as if they were looking directly at me. like it was some delicious secret only the two of us were sharing. I was immediately in love with all of them. I finally understood what my mother was so angry about. these were the women she had been yelling about for years. the whores my father had left us for. suddenly I couldn't blame him. I would have left my mother for them too. they were intoxicating. I still didn't understand the basic mechanics of sex, but I knew the photographs were stirring a terrible heat in my crotch. Pablo had mentioned something about putting your dick inside their pussies, but I was confused about how that was supposed to work. it wasn't long before all my uncles were waiting in line outside the door. taking turns in there. they had devised an elaborate system. no more than ten minutes before you had to give it up to let the next in line have their turn. I waited in line, but the fuckers never let me in. they laughed at me every time I tried to slip in there. *what the fuck are you gonna do?* shit, I didn't know there was anything you were supposed *to do* in there. It really got me

195

thinking. one day, Pablo left and forgot to padlock the door behind him. I waited patiently for everyone to take off to summer school and then slipped in. It was amazing. all those pretty women, naked and looking right at me. I could see their tits. man….it was really something. I thought about what Pablo had said: *what the fuck are you gonna do?* I had to do something, but what? how? I noticed my little dick was hard so I grabbed at it for a bit, but nothing came of it. after a while, I left. as I climbed the few steps up, I found uncle Oldemar on the other side of the door. He was laughing his ass off. I don't know why, but I got embarrassed. my cheeks flushing with heat. I fucking hated him. I really felt something important had happened. Like I had learned something. Oldemar's laughing lessened it somehow. I hated him for that. I wanted to fucking kill him. That was it, he had gone too far. some shit you just weren't supposed to do and laughing at me about that was one of them. I vowed to kill him. I didn't know he was schizophrenic then. no one did. that came later. back then, he was just crazy Oldemar and I was going to fucking kill him. and I knew just how I would do it, too.

another 90 days

wait, fuck,
I think it's the cops
fuck, hold up
shit
I'm getting
pulled over
stash the weed
fuck
look, my license
is suspended
and I got priors
so,
I'm going to
jail
call Annette for me
alright?
see if the cops
will let you
drive my truck
home
fuck
I guess I'll see
you guys
later
license,
registration
and proof of insurance
please
yeah…
here's the
thing.

do that stuff

Kimba told me about
the night she met
George Clinton.
he invited her into
his trailer
but he smelled
fucking terrible
and the whole
place was so thick
with crack smoke
it was actually
hard for her
to breathe.
she said it was
disgusting,
but I still thought
it was cool,
because fucking
GEORGE CLINTON
right?
but today
I find myself
worrying
about him.
hoping he's being
mindful of his age
and laying off
the shit
a little bit.
I just feel better
knowing
he's out there
somewhere,
doing
his thing,
you know?
but then
I got to

thinking
that
whatever
he is,
and has
had to be,
all these
years,
to get to
the funk
and lay it
down
on the one
is a mystery
too vast
and powerful
for anyone
to question
so
fuck it,
hit that shit
George,
cause funk
not only
moves,
it can
re-move,
dig?

problems

the problem
with drinking
is the same as
the problem
with fucking
after you've had
too much to drink.
the problem
with love,
is the same as
the problem
with death.

the problem
with your knee
when it's cold
and damp
is just like
the problem
with the memory
of the time you had to
walk home in the rain
after your best friend
drove off with the girl
you wanted to fuck so bad
it actually hurt your dick.

the problem with
still being on acid
at four in the morning
when your back starts
to hurt and the beer
has zero effect
has much
in common with
the problem with
being too fat
to get your dick

properly in her mouth
while you
finger her standing up
with one hand
and try to
twist her nipples
with the other,
and this
is a serious problem.

all this would be
so much easier
if I didn't
over think it
but that's always
been
my biggest
problem:

thinking,

despite
all my
vain attempts
to put a stop
to it.

even this,
right now,

I nearly
thought it
and myself
to death

broken dolls

tell me where you kept
your broken dolls,
after you'd
gouged out their eyes,
and cut off their hair.
tell me how far back
you stuffed them
into the corners
you thought
no one could find.
tell me how you
cut off their dresses
and drew on their faces,
how you
lied to everyone
about where
they had gone.
knowing now
these dolls
were you,
knowing now
you'd something
to prove
and you sure
showed them
didn't you?

tell me how
you learned
to forget
what you did,
how you smiled
and kept secret,
the things
that you hid.
I want to know this
about you,
this secret self

you hurt
then hide away.
I want to know
her
and all the other
selves
you swear
you never
meant
to be

tell me
and I swear
to keep it
secret.

tell me
because
you know
that I
can
keep
a secret.

like memory

under roots
in the
deep earth
where shadows
hide things
that slither
like memory
sliding off
good-good
drugs

a slipstream

serpents
breaking
down to
worms,
in the earth
the deep
beneath,
where living
things
hide
from light

and the day
that breaks
like those
first bones
did,
that pain
the fucking
surprise,
light
dancing
in wilderness
eyes

under roots
where trees
hold tight.
dead leaves,
rotting
down to
lakebed

heavy
like memory
changing

all night blood
and silvery
cream

and the
moon
finally
answering
questions

it's late
and what
about it?
she asks
lying naked
on the floor

night birds
swooping
down
silent
as fog
thinking:

they're
hungry

and
so
am

I

the good ole days

there was a time when
I really had to work
at getting my eyes
on a naked woman.
there were precious few
options

I could,
save up for a whore,
or shoplift
a dirty magazine
from the pharmacy
in Hollywood

fantasizing
for weeks.
wondering
if I'd ever
work up the nerve
to approach
one of those
smiling
Sunset blvd-whores.
or what the next
stolen HUSTLER
would have
inside.
even where
I would hide
the magazine
added something
to it.
back then
a moment
of lasciviousness
was a rare
and
powerful

thing.
something
to look forward to
in an otherwise
vacant
and pointless
existence.

now the whores
have gone
deep into the
recesses
of escort sites
and online
dating,
and dirty magazines
barely exist.

now with
the internet
it's all so
instant
so ordinary
like buying
orange juice
or looking
out the window.

and ordinary
just isn't
sexy

inevitable

death comes
for everyone.
people die
around you
so you can prepare.
get your affairs
in order.
murder and
suicide
make death
trickier than
it already is.
when death
brushes up
against you,
questions of
faith arise.
answer these
make a choice.
death is not
limited to loss
it can
sometimes
branch off
into
horror,
and terror
(see murder & suicide)
whatever the case,
it's inevitable.
one day,
death comes.
sometimes
it lingers
sometimes not.
seldom pleasant.
like dentistry
or car repairs.

it's odd that death
can make a person
feel isolated
and alone..
when in fact,
it is one of the
few things,
we can all share,
it's important
to remember:
intoxication
is mini-death.
death in moderation.
It's the best way
to do it,
if you can
manage
just a bit
of dignity

running

I'm a lucky man.
lots of people
love me,
good, kind people.
I have laughter
and excitement
in my life.
I get out a lot
and have meaningful
experiences,
I have a beautiful son
two beautiful stepchildren
four beautiful grandchildren
caring and sensitive siblings
and a wife that has surpassed
all of my
most generous
expectations.

I have a good life.

some mornings
usually while driving to work,
I burst into tears
weeping at the sheer miracle
of my good fortune.

yet, there is this
persistent thought
that haunts me:

*you are a bad person
and don't deserve any of this,
one day,
you will find a way
to destroy it.*
I don't know where
that comes from,

but wherever it is
I've been running
from it
all my life

and now
there's apparently
some thing
seriously wrong
with my
leg.

to die

I don't
want to die
in an expensive
hospital
looking up at
synthetic light
glowing out of
white glass tubes
manufactured
by people
slaved into
submission,
in countries
where
subjugation
is a welcome
respite
from starvation

I don't want
to die
in a car crash
looking up
at crooked trees
through thousands
of tiny cracks
in a windshield
when I die
I don't want
the wind
shielded

I hope,
when I get
old enough,
all that's left
to harness
is love.

I hope the love
is seeded
by the
breakdown
of anger

I don't want
to die
in an American
National Park,
clutching
my chest
with my
contorted face
twitching up
toward an
American
sky

because there is no
America
in the sky

when I die
I want someone
to smile,
I want
someone
to be relieved
even if
it's me,
especially
if it's me

conversation

you said:
it just means,
that you have
a purpose,
and you can't
be mad
at that
and I said:
no, but
I can be
surprised
by how much
it hurts.

inertia

feeling
too old for fire,
perhaps the fight
has left me.
sitting on my couch,
planning ahead.
the tags on the car
are due,
fucking thing
won't pass the
smog check.
the dentist has been calling
because he knows
my teeth are rotting
in my skull.
have to make
an appointment
with the doctor,
my prescriptions
are up.
sitting on the couch
with a limp dick
in my lap,
worrying about the cats,
and the leaky faucet
in the kitchen.
I've broken two toes
in the last
two months.
what the fuck
I keep tripping over,
is a fucking mystery.
I want to get up already,
but to go where?
to do what?

about time

my son, almost thirteen
lost in dick jokes
and toilet humor,
the mark of his age,
nights spent
eyeing each other
from opposite ends
of the couch,
fighting for the
remote,
cracking each other
up,
and talking shit
like old friends
on the porch.
last year we
shared a drink
on new year's eve,
yesterday, we laughed
as some disturbing shit
on the television.

my mind
drifting back to
the sheer miracle of
having someone
call you
father
and have it mean
something
to both of you.
reflecting
on all the moments
I never shared
with *my* father
him, always
too busy
with his new wife

or his new kids,
or a shiny
new pussy
to slide his
his dick in.
but recently
there's been
a curious absence
of bitterness
as my son grows
into a kind
young man.
knowing that
what we've shared
is a type of healing
of forgiving…
because now
I'm
more father
than son,
belonging
to someone
from the
other side
of need and want
even love.
forever turning
the strange
hands of time.
my shoulder
suddenly something
to look up to
rather than to
look over.

she worries about me

I'm home now,
you can call off
the dogs.
I know,
I was drunk,
I stopped
in McArthur park
to look for some
coke
don't worry
I didn't find any,
I don't know why
I always forget:
nobody
sells powder
in the street
anymore.
but listen,
it's all good
I got a
couple rocks.
I'll just
crumple them
over the weed
in your pipe,
ok?
hey?
where you going?
don't you want
to party?

the source

there was a piss smell in the bathroom.
no matter how hard I scrubbed the toilet
or mopped the floor, I could not eradicate
this smell. It was driving me crazy…well,
crazy-*er*. maybe it's me, I thought…so
I sniffed at my underwear, my pajama shorts
my shoes and my slippers. maybe my dick
is rotting, I thought. maybe there are urine
deposits in my urethra? I couldn't figure it out
and it was no small problem. I am cursed by
an olfactory prowess that seldom manifests
in pleasant forms. after several months,
I gave up on identifying the source of the odor.
another annoyance I must learn to live with,
I reasoned. but today, something happened.
after scoring a handful of my favorite pills,
I came home elated by the lack of pain in
my damaged leg. so I decided to clean
the bathroom. first the sink, the shower,
toilet and then the floor. as I began mopping
the tile around the base of the toilet,
I heard a sound. the mop had caught something
that clanked to the floor.
I bent over and picked it up. at first, I couldn't
make out what it was. just this brown hunk
of metal that felt alien in my hand. then I saw
a post with some threading and knew it was
a bolt. but the head of it was caked in some
kind of brown residue. naturally, I picked at it
with my fingernails, and a large clump came
loose. that's when it hit me: a powerful blast
of concentrated piss-stink so intense I
almost fell over. it was strong. panicking,
I rushed to the sink to wash my hands,
but the shit had gotten under my
nails. I cannot begin to describe the revulsion
I felt. I almost threw up. just the thought of it:
my mop had dislodged a toilet bolt that was

covered in some kind of urine deposits. a
fucking bouillon bolt of concentrated piss
matter. I immediately thought of soup
or tea. I almost threw up again. I washed
my hands over and over, trying to get
that shit out from under my nails. but I kept
using my nails, to get it out from under
my nails, and it was just spreading. I'd
never seen anything like it. it was like trying
to wash resin out of a weed pipe
the more you washed, the more everywhere
it got. I swear I almost had a breakdown.
how did I get here? sweating , panting
and dry heaving into the sink, with my nails
covered in piss-smear? all I wanted to do was
clean. I almost started crying but then, something
occurred to me: ..... I had found it. the *source*.
after all those weeks frantically sniffing into
the furthest corners of my imagination, I had
found it. knowing then, it was almost over.
knowing soon, I'd never have to smell it again.
I was overcome with joy. I washed the piss bolt
with pine-sol and alcohol. I did the same with
my nails. eventually the brown started to fade.
I began to feel lighter. a new perspective,
seemed to be forming. a new day dawning,
if you will. after thirty eight, hard fought
minutes, it was over. you can't imagine
how clean I felt. purified, really. cleansed.
then I looked up into the mirror. this was
a mistake. I was drenched in sweat and a
very strange smile had spread across my face.
it was unlike any, I had seen before.
I considered dwelling on that, but thought
better of it. I allowed myself to be pleased with
what I had done. I returned to the living room,
triumphant. Annette had fallen asleep
on the couch. I considered waking her, such was
my excitement, but I decided against it.
what would I say to her? how could I explain?

baby, guess what happened in the bathroom?
instead, I just sat down, and really started to
wonder about what the fuck, might actually be
wrong with me.

more than Huxley

remembering
that first time
on Mescaline.
the taste
in my throat,
because Julian
had convinced
all of us to
break open the
capsules and snort it.

the way the cars
parked in the street
began to bounce
and I
couldn't stop
laughing..
how Hugo was
freaking out
and no one
was surprised.

remembering
that weird guy
that lived in the
old jail museum,
that strange old
building,
made of stones
and bars.
how he showed us
his giant
drawing pad,
filled with
multi-colored
paintings of Jesus
page after page
filled with

psychedelic
Christs
with hair
that wouldn't
stop moving,
and how he told us
his name was
E-TER-BA

and Hugo
just laughing
and laughing,
uncontrollably
on the lawn
outside.
that crazy kid
we invited
that was also
named Dennis
and how wise
and serene
he proved
to be
guiding us
through the trip
like an ancient
guru, keeping us
all calm
and assuring us
that it was all
just part of the trip..

we were all just sixteen
but I felt
much older
than that.

and although
I was scared
and baffled

by everything
and everyone
around me
I knew something
important
was happening,
just as I knew
I would never
forget it
or ever,
be the same.
I was right
just like
Huxley
more
than
Huxley.

mis-led

to think that
all that time
I thought
it was
me.
the drug
terror,
the fear
nestling
in like
a pack
of rabid
dogs
circling
a space
I thought
I had
all to myself.
so many
bad trips
that seemed
eternal
and somehow
deserved.
enduring
one disaster
after
another.
misreading
all the signs,
.
all that guilt
for what
I had
done to them
but I don't
blame them,
everybody

needs
a devil
to blame,
besides,
I was the one
that had read
all those
scary books.
I was the one
with a coffin
and a six foot
a crucifix
in my room.
I don't mind
that they
blamed
me…
but for
years
I believed
them
I thought
it was all
about me
and that was
really just a
serious
waste
of
fucking
time.

older, wiser

It might not seem
like a big deal,
but it took me
twenty years
to be able
to turn down
a line of coke.
twenty years
to gain
enough foresight
to see
far enough
into the night
where I'm
snorting
the last bit
off the plate,
and asking
myself:
what the fuck
did you
do that for?
the inevitable
paranoid
sweating.
the terrible
feeling
of sudden
panic.
praying
for a sleep
that won't come
for hours.
cursing the
first glint
of dawn,
with my head
pounding

and my heart
racing.

now, when
someone offers
me a line,
I can smile
and simply say
nah, I'm good.
and though
it may not sound
like a huge
accomplishment,
for me,
it's monumental.
one of the few
perks
of getting
older.
that,
and knowing
there's
no such thing
as free
pussy
or classic
rock

innocence

the first time
hands
other
than your own
touch your sex,
is like
a revelation.
a thrill beyond
compare.
unfortunately
you can never
choose,
whose hands
those will be.
or how old
you are,
or the fact
that it might
haunt you
for the
rest
of your
life.
and therein
lies the question:
if you could
change
that first time,
as inappropriate
as it might have
been,
would you?

redemption no

the secret meeting
with my
dead mother
and my
dead grandmother,
in that dingy
motel room
with the
dark green
curtains....
knowing
deep down
how impossible
it was,
wanting
to scream:
but you're
dead!
what are you
doing here?
the pain
in their eyes
wet with tears
and afraid
to look up
at me
why won't
you fucking
look at me?
you have to
forgive him
they said
as if
ashamed
to even
bring him up
but I wouldn't
couldn't

angry
that
that
was
all
they wanted
to say
to me

stumbling
into a bright
day that felt
punishing,
a sunlight
that seemed
dark
and relentless,
my dumb legs
limping into
a busy
intersection
and the asphalt
melting
beneath
my soft
shoes
a pool
of melting
street
like tar
sucking
the dinosaur
of my dim
confusion
and their
weeping
eyes
looking at me,
from that
terrible room

knowing then,
this is
what kills me,
this is how
I die.
and all I
can think
is:
fuck him,
I'll NEVER
let it go,
he killed
my mother,
it was
worth it,
as the flames
lick
at my heels
and the
liquid
street
swallows me
whole.

glory

I like it
when she
crawls naked
on the bed.
her haunches
flexing
as her ass
opens just enough
to make the world
disappear.

I like it when
she looks over
her shoulder,
and her eyes
drop to my center
smiling,
pleased

and I'm constantly
amazed
that I get
to witness
her
in all
her
glory

how
did I
get
so lucky?
oh, right,
it isn't
luck

no small victory

remember
that it was
you
that asked
me
to put it
in your ass,
but it was
also you
that asked
me
to pull it
out
because
you just
couldn't
take it.
so remember
that when
you
asked *me*
to move
out of
my apartment,
it was
not
actually
your victory
when *I*
decided
to leave.

realization

It's not like I planned on buying a ten rock at nine in the morning on a Wednesday. these were the perils of being a messenger: too much free time to drive around and think. and it's not like I didn't know what the brother on the corner meant when he nodded at me in my car, I just pulled over, lost in reckless addict auto pilot. before I realized what had happened, I had pulled away with crack in my hand, still wet from the dealer's saliva. I set it on the passenger seat to dry while I dug in the glove compartment for my weed pipe. I thought about circling back to pick up a straight-shooter but didn't want to push my luck with the cops. luckily, there was still some weed in the bowl. I broke a piece off the rock and crumpled it over the weed, taking a giant blast while driving down Main Street. man, what a fucking RUSH. within seconds, I was paranoid and plotting where, and how I would take my next hit. it was a god awful feeling. nothing else mattered. I had some documents to file at the superior court for work and the thought of it was filling me with dread. where would I park? how far would I have to walk? how long was the line going to be? when the fuck was I going to be able to take my next blast? the rock seemed pretty big for ten bucks, and I was excited about how many hits I might get out of it. soon I was parking and folding the rock into an old receipt, careful not to crumble it. I packed the lighter and my pipe into my pocket and headed over to the courthouse. my heart was beating like crazy. I panicked when I saw the metal detectors but then remembered my weed pipe was glass. I was so happy I had decided to buy a glass pipe. I waited in line, nervously eyeing the sheriffs. putting my lighter and keys into the tray, I made it through the detector and felt an elation more beautiful than love. I stopped at the trashcan to come up with a solid plan. I decided on taking a blast in the bathroom before waiting in line to file my documents. maybe I could flag down one of my courthouse friends, and cut to the front of the line? I thought about this as I sat, with my pants at my ankles in the handicap stall of the 2nd fl men's room. with my documents resting on my lap, I carefully unfolded the receipt and broke off another piece of the sacred rock. after loading the pipe, I gathered my thoughts. it was important that I light *only* the crack. if some of the weed began to burn, someone might smell it and report it, but I was confident I could pull off the maneuver. I lit the piece gently and inhaled an enormous amount of smoke, careful to hold it in for as long as possible. just then *a fucking county sheriff* walked in. I could hear his keys jangling, and his radio squawking. I peered through the crack in the door, just to make sure. it was a sheriff alright. still holding in the hit, I panicked. knowing if I exhaled he would smell it. knowing if I didn't, I would pass out. in a fury, I pulled off my shirt as quietly as I could, and exhaled the giant blast into it. I don't think I had ever been more afraid. after I was done, I waited a beat and put my shirt back on, all the while peering through the crack in the door. hoping to god he would not take a look into my stall. he didn't, and after a few more squawks of his radio he left. the relief I felt cannot be measured. I sat for a moment marveling at my luck *and* my stupidity. how the fuck I ever thought that smoking crack in the L.A. Superior Court was a good idea, was beyond me. after I filed my documents and got back to my car, I immediately began to plan for my next hit. I decided that I should finish whatever I had left, while driving in the car. that's when the FEAR came. it was bad. my hands began to shake, and my eyes began to dart. I was positive the sheriffs were back there, following me. I kept frantically checking my mirrors, convinced cop lights were going to light me up any second. I realized then I had made the worst mistake of my life. my heart was pounding in my chest. I knew there were only two possible outcomes: I was either: going to die, or I was: going to jail. I couldn't decide which would be worse so I pulled over and called Annette. I would have been crying but the shit was too strong to let the tears come. Surprisingly, she was not moved by my story.

"What the fuck Dennis?
You call me at work
cause you're freaking out
on crack, and I'm supposed to
what? Tell you everything is
going to be ok? Fuck you Dennis,
I'm at work, you're on your own."

I was devastated. I hopped on the freeway and took my last six hits driving west, on the 10. I couldn't feel them anymore. it was like the coke was broken. *I deserve this* I thought. for being a bitch. I wish I could say I never smoked crack again, but I can't. I will say this though, it was never the same after that. I only did it another handful of times, but it was always a disappointment. something about the disgust in Annette's voice. I never forgot it, and I still can't.

forgot something in the car

I hurt my arm,
I don't know
I just saw that it was
bleeding, and after I
saw,
that it was
bleeding,
it started to hurt,
you know?
I went to reach
into the car,
I don't know
for my flannel
or a gallon of
water
some shit
but you know,
as I leaned in there
my arm reached for
the edge of the car
for balance
and I just,
missed it
and suddenly
I was falling
into the back seat
of my own car
flailing on my back
like some self-rape
scenario of,
I don't know.
my glasses
almost broke
and were hanging
on my face all
half on half off
so I couldn't
see straight

and I got turned
all upside down,
and the edge of
my arm, must have
scraped against,
the edge of my car
and anyway
now it's bleeding
and the edging on
my car came loose
and I had to, you know
re-tuck all that fucking
spaghetti....but listen
I don't want you to worry
or anything, it's just in case
you see BLOOD
because
I know blood can,
I know blood will sometimes
you know,
blood,
I know blood.

but the thing is,
that got me worried
because I fell, but I don't
really remember
falling, I was just
kind of upside down
all of a sudden
and it took me
a few seconds
to even figure out
where I was or what
had happened
because time did that thing
that time does sometimes
where it just skips a bit
and you're not sure *when*
it is anymore

anyway
I started to worry that
I might have
suffered a little stroke,
just a little one, not like
your arm going numb
and you can't speak
but just,
so I came upstairs to look
in the mirror because I heard
or read somewhere that if you
thought you had a stroke
you should look
into a mirror and smile
and if your lips can't do it
and half your face is drooping
chances are you
had a stroke and it
occurred to me
as I stood there
smiling into
the god damn mirror:
hey, you're doing
a stroke-check
in the mirror.
what the fuck Dennis?
but you know,
there was also
the mushrooms
and by then
I was really feeling,
you know,
the mushrooms
were really starting to
and things had gotten
real....just a lot of
extra,
I don't know
happening
so much new

things seemed
to be...
but listen
that's a story
for another
time.

never ceases

the elders,
watered down
their skin wrinkling
veins cooling
hands curling into
little fists.

it's an opening
death hymn

tears to wet
the earth
when the
rain forgets

the light when
the shadows
give in
to the sun

lit by that

and if the gods
were here
they would
laugh

listening

tiny altars
peering out
broken
windows

I don't
belong
to this
am a part of it

only
to witness
to testify

people
beaten into
a mass
of red foam

the clock turns,
leans
suddenly stops
arms
reaching
into the
very last second
hands closing
into
final gestures
nails
scratching
last words
into
the sky

the sky
that
never

ceases.

as good a time
as any
to die

hoochie-coochie man

I was
six years
old,
so was she.
Darla was
the grand daughter
of the fat old
black lady
that lived upstairs.
it was just
the two of them
living up there
and this scared me.
where were her
parents?
my dad had
recently left us
so all I had
was my mother
and worried
that she might
leave too.
I thought
Darla was
the prettiest girl
I had ever seen.
you wanna see
something funny?
she asked me
one Tuesday morning,
sure, I said.
so I followed her
to the garage
around back.
we're gonna do
the hoochie coochie!
she said, then quickly
bent over and

pulled down
her little pants
and pointed
her bubbly ass
cheeks
at me.
now you gotta
take off your pants
and put your
pee-pee
in my butt.
I didn't get it
but went for it
anyway.
like this
I asked?
yeah, but you gotta
put it in there!
my little peewee
just grazed her
pretty butt cheek
and it was over.
she quickly
pulled up
her pants
and declared:
we did the hoochie coochie!
I felt proud
and noticed
that my
tiny penis
was hard.
it was weird
but I felt
like something
important
had happened.
but then
we had
to move

when my mother
finally gave up
on waiting
for my dad
to come back.
I never saw
Darla again,
but I never forgot her.
even now
I still remember.
looking back
I wonder:
where did she learn
about that?
how did
a six year old girl
come to believe
that a penis
should be
put inside
a girl's butt?
I wonder
why she was
living with her
grandmother.
I wonder what happened
to her?
I know what
happened to me
just a few months
later.

ordinary

a crowd had gathered
at the base of the building.
a woman had crawled out
onto a window washer's
scaffolding,
she must have been
at least
24 stories up
she was dressed in an
old, dirty night gown
and she was screaming,
screaming and
cackling this terrible
manic laugh.
though I couldn't hear
what she was saying,
she was obviously
hurling insults
down to the curious group
of people down below.
she had this crazy hair
that was billowing
around her face.
there was something
wrong with her face
her mouth was covered
in a dark ring that looked like
charcoal or old blood

after some time
the crowd began to lose
patience
and began yelling at her
why don't you just jump
you crazy bitch?
yeah jump!
soon it became a chant:
jump, jump, JUMP! JUMP!

and suddenly
I was angry with her.
who did she think she was?
freaking out up there,
making a scene
and fucking with the
morning traffic?
I was tired of it.
why didn't she just
jump, and get it
over with already?
what a fucking coward,
frustrated
I decided to join in
on the chant
and angrily yelled up:
JUMP!
and just like that,
she did.
fucking leapt out of
that scaffolding
and came flying down
at us…at *me*
arms flailing,
legs kicking
and she was still
screaming
and laughing.

about half way down
I could just make out
what she was saying
don't leave me!
don't leave me!
that's when I realized
it was my mother.
and she was
looking
right at me
with tears streaming

down the sides
of her face.
and then she hit
the ground
and split
my heart,
wide open.
I woke up screaming
with tears
running down
my face.
It was the worst
nightmare
I had ever had.

I don't know
how or why
but
I knew then
she *would*
kill herself
one day,
and then
ten years later
she did,
and it was
otherwise
just another
ordinary
day.
like today.

what has the world come to?

driving through
Inglewood,
I noticed two
white police officers
on motorcycles,
pull up next to me.
I had a brief flash of fear,
but then remembered:
I'm old now
and I don't have any
real drugs, in the car,
no warrants looming
over me,
shit…even my insurance
and tags were paid
I stole a few glances
and noticed what
looked like small
assault rifles
jutting out of
custom holsters
built into their bikes.
the light turned green
and they sped up
and passed me
quickly flashing
their lights at the
beat up van, just ahead
I slowed down
relieved that it wasn't me
a half block ahead
the van pulled over
and I noticed something
coming out of the window,
as I passed the van.
it was a pair
of dark, wrinkled hands.
working hands

calloused and splattered
with paint ...
and they were *shaking*.
as I passed the van
I looked inside and saw
an old black man,
wearing an old
baseball cap,
head lowered,
obviously afraid.
I thought: damn,
is this what time it is?
does he really need to be
that careful?
I drove on
and went about
my business.

later,
I made the mistake
of listening to news
on the radio,
and I thought,
yeah, he does
need to be that careful,
that afraid.

but I won't ask:
what has the world
come to?
because it hasn't come
to anything,
it hasn't
changed at all.

knowing better

I am that thing
that lurks
in the shadow
cast by my own
subtle deformities.

the thing
that waits
in the stillness,

biding its time

and knowing
just when
to slither in.

sometimes
I'll catch a glimpse
on a window,
or in a mirror.

I try to
ignore it,
to pretend
the dark of me
isn't coming,
even though
I know better,
even though
knowing,
changes
nothing.

there I am

watching him,
the lines
in his face
creasing.
watching him,
drunk,
smiling
not leering yet,
but close

laughter
leaning into
violence

getting into
the car,
late night
submarine sandwich
consolation.

the drunk of him
driving fast
the danger of it

locked in a
moving cage,
with a
rabid animal.

watching him
looking for signs
looking real close
looking for reasons
looking
for me.

respect

I heard my name
being shouted
from the street
just beneath
my hotel window.
It was Beast.
well, it was Shaon,
but he wanted
everyone to
call him Beast
ay Dennis!
so I leaned out,
yo Dennis!
give me a ride
real quick!
I knew it
was trouble,
so I grabbed
my keys.
where we going
fool?
up by Alvarado
so I took 7th
and made a right
down Alvarado
couple blocks up
he says:
ay, pull up right here.
so I did and noticed
he was waving
someone over.
a dark little
central-american dude
walked up,
he had long hair and an
Iron Maiden shirt
definitely *MARA*
real quick I could

hear Beast
asking him for a twenty
so he leans into
the passenger window
and pulls a rock
out of his mouth
and places it in his
open palm
wet with spit.
the spit didn't
bother me at all
if you've ever
smoked crack
you know why.
so Beast tells him,
that shit's tiny fool
you got any bigger one's?
so the guy pulls out a
couple more.
serio? those are tiny!
that's all you got?
so the guys pulls out
three more.
captivated.
I can't take my eyes off
the six big rocks
all wet and sticky in
homie's hand.
Suddenly,
ever so gently
as if in slow motion,
Beast just
swats his hand down
and all the rocks
just tumble into
the car.
ay, you better drive fool.
I floor it in first gear
peeling out and looking
into my rearview mirror.

I can hear some
real angry Spanish
and I see two other
homies running up.
hands are waving
there's a lot of screaming,
two guns are drawn
but no one shoots.
my heart is beating
so hard I swear
I can hear it.
What the fuck man?
and I can't tell if
I'm angry or excited.
relax fool,
you know how
much money those
bitches make?
they budget
for this kind of shit.

and suddenly
I respected him.
I was in awe.
and that was just
the first time
I thought
I was going to die
that night.

thanks for the advice, *man*

don't be
so sensitive
don't be such a
fucking coward
be a fucking man
man the fuck up.
you have to show em
who's boss,
you have to show em
who's in charge.
don't be a pussy,
if they hit you,
hit em back.
never walk away
from a fight.
fight your way
out.
never let a bitch
tell you
what to do.
keep her ass
in check.
if your kids
talk back
hit em,
hit em hard,
so they
don't forget.
act and walk
like *a man*.
don't be a *puto*.

as above

a tangle of veins
pushing up
thin skin
oily
and reflecting
dingy
yellow
light

panties
tossed
sexy
on the
bathroom
tiles

and the moonlight
hits the river
just where she
starts to
turn

a frothing
heaving mass
of wet

a little taste,
the dark
that beckons
tourniquet love
bound in
leather

and the flies
come fast
to the feast
of famine

tonight
before
the light
brings
ruin

what the clerics
knew
and hid

something
slithering
in the swamp

a cool vendetta
robed.
redemption,
another way
out
poised in
shadow

above

the stars

below

the stars

fading

I miss her
in my bones,
when I'm breathing
heavy
it gets on my clothes.
remembering
her smile.
I drive by
the last place
I saw her.
sometimes I stop
and park the car.
on my way home
from work,
sometimes
I take 8th street,
and drive by our
old houses,
trying to conjure up
pleasant memories
but there aren't
that many.
mostly I just
remember
the rats in the attic
and her bedroom door
always locked.

every now and then
I'll catch myself
doing something
that she
would have done,
the way I wipe
the hair
from my son's
face,
or when

I'm cleaning my glasses
in the car,
using a little washcloth
I keep
tucked to the side
of the parking brake.

I can't help
but wish
she could've met
Henry.
she would have
loved him
so much,
it hurts to think
about it.
but I do,
every time
I see him smile,
every time
he says
something stupid
and makes me
laugh.

I miss her
so much,
sometimes
it feels
like I can't even
breathe.
but I can,
and I do,
despite
the weight
on my chest.
what choice
do I have?

lately, I've come

to cherish
those moments,
when the hurt
just washes over me.

because I know
it's all I have left
of her.

I worry that
one day
I won't even
have that.

one day
she'll just
fade away,

like everyone
does.

like you
did.

important call

like blood
glistening
on a vulture's
head
it's hungry
eyes
fixing on
the death feast,
wet beneath
it's claws

the
sweet scent
of carrion
sickening
the air :

that's
how it feels
every time
the phone
rings

and I'm
hoping
someone
is calling
to tell me
you're
finally
dead.

puzzle of cells in transit

the soft and
easily molded
masses,
taken by the glow of
abject consumerism
and the hollow
promise of ownership

the poor and
disenfranchised,
wanting and suffering,
living out slow
and painful
lives of need
and neglect

the entitled,
comfortable and only
a little guilty.
afraid to
publicly boast
of their
constant pleasure
and limitless
resource
happily rejoicing
in the secrecy
of their
elite and
very private
circles

poets
cast aside,
isolated and
driven mad
by circumstance,
addiction,

and genetic
pre-disposition

angry
sociopaths
climbing
on the backs
of the meek
to their
universally respected
perches
of power

predatory clergy
awash in their
self-prescribed
sanctity
feeding on worship,
adulation and
illicit sex

all just
a puzzle
of cells
teeming
in the sick
sea of a
simian
fantasy
that is
finally

almost
over.

by choice

falling forward.
no shadow
but the after-light
of leaving.
not spinning,
just a slow,
and purposeful
descent
into the soft
surrender
of the
cold hard floor.
a home
more than
any other.
my head
welcoming
the dull thud,
my face
eager to split
and bruise.
and so,
I let go
finally sure
of something,
finally
at peace,
with
just
one
choice

self-entwined

pink dolphins
in the paintings
an abstract
approach
to convey
that one
telepathic
conversation
because
no one
believes you
none of them
can agree
the group
circling
the anomaly
flopping
on the beach

a cluster of minds
already
somewhere else
home later
telling friends
at work about it

the cold sun
shrugging
not at all
surprised

there were
so many police
at the bakery
this morning
something
starting early,
rising with

the bread

the iridescent
snakes
looking
right at you.
so many of them
with ears.
the re-occurring
space:
tiled floors,
marble pillars,
and the river
of dark.

real because
you've *been*
there

Ayahuasca
growing quietly
in the
jungle dark
self-entwined

a vegetable mind
appealing
to the meat heavy
heart

just listen
a voice says
and you do
because you
trust it
and that
doesn't come easy

just listen
and you do

because
the animals
are changing
shape
and we're
becoming
them

thirty thousand years
we've been
giving our heads
to them
retelling plant lessons
their elaborate
ceremonies
a necessary
release
from language

so many more
minds
than mine

restless,
waiting
to connect

tuning my frequency

I'm here,
I'm ready.

compromise

an idea
emerging,
like opening
a window,
to let the light in,
or a heart
to let the hurt
out

sloughing off
the burden
of toil
with vice

flirting with madness,
fingering psychosis

coaxing shadows
from the corners
of the room
something to
dance with later
when the night
get long

aging fingers
circling
where there
used
to be hair,
a smooth
head
covering
a battered
mind
scars of
thinking

crisscrossing
just beneath
the skin

despair
then
a door
a way out

perhaps

another
way in

and like this
a compromise
with infinity
is reached
not:
just in time
but close

don't spit

remember
the night,
remember
and respect
the moon.
you are
but a speck
on the blight
of existence,
no more
important
than a
particle
of dust
or a
sperm stain
on
the bathroom
tiles

knowing
your role
in the
grand scheme
of things
will make
the idiocy
of being
that much
easier
to swallow

that much
easier
to end.

the sparrow

perhaps
the sparrow,
a dented eye
turned up
against the noise
of the city.
perhaps a hawk.
a trembling
that will not
subside.
perhaps a crow
pulling wings
like capes
over the
glaring sun.
in that shadow,
perhaps.
a perfect
melody
of mourning,
finally
in the light
of day

the sacrosanctity
of a final
zero
the end leaning
against
a luminous
now.

and here
the eyes
let go,
here
the wind
sings,

lest the wings
falter,
lest doubt
win

a particle
dancing
in ephemeral
breeze
the universe
winking
a sly
reprise

perhaps
the sparrow,
folding trees.
the seeing
closing eyes,
falling
to their knees

perhaps
the raven
flying in our
night clothes.
wearing,
flying and
knowing
everything
we
don't
want it
to.

let's

I want to
dress up with you.
c'mon
you be fascist
and I'll be
shade.

get your
heels sharpened
before the parade

I want to
go with you
to the war

help
you fight
all the
enemies
and some
of our friends

I want to get up
with you
early
like you
always say
is good for us

take me to work
to the job
you hate.
I want to shit
what you ate
there
c'mon
you be alligator
and I'll be bait.

both of us
can wait.
we can
take our time
because it's ours
to take
wait
show me
that again
how you were
back then
the part of you
that remembers
what most of you
forgets

the accident
in the car

I want to be
the one rolling
into the dirt
coming to,
pregnant
and bruised

you be informant
and I'll be muse

we can kick up
something
both of us
can use

just **a dream?**

it would be different
if so much of it
hadn't come true,
hadn't come to pass.
(past?)
easier to dispel
had I not beared
(bared?)
witness

with my own eyes
as they say

and sure
I only *dreamed*
an inanimate
sentient orb
that explained
how I had
complexity
all wrong,
how it was
not to revere
or worship,
but to translate,
and simplify.
all the while
shape shifting,
retracting
and extending

an impossible
challenge to absolutes

because they're
traps
it said
because we're maps

that no one's read
it explained
and led me
to know
and oh
the relief of this
word-free
communication
not lost
on my so-called-writer
selves.
like the warmth
of sex
that's finally
right
the right way
with the *only*
person
taking my hand
and pulling
it over
pulling it in
pulling it
close.

sure it was
just a dream
but that's
happened
to me now
I've seen it
with my own
eyes,
closed.

you were screaming

why do I
dream about
cleavers?

*because you keep reading
books about
all those killers
then obsess about
how they cut
into the meat
of people*

*cutting people
while
they're still
alive
and screaming,*

*remember
when you were
screaming?*

why the
ceaseless questions
about coincidence?

*that shit will
make you crazy.*

*forget that man,
why are you
paying
so much
attention
to that?*

*are you hungry?
what's happening?*

you used to
be hungry
all the time

what's happening
with time?

why do I believe
there will never
be an end
to questions?

you can't put
that shit on me,
you were like that
when I met you.
you've
always
been
like that

you're supposed to
shake it off,
when you wake up.
you're supposed to be
OK when you realize
it was all just a dream.

but you're not
are you?
and that's
happened to you
now,
hasn't it?

stakes

do we
ultimately
create
who we are,
or is that
done
for us?
the answer
perhaps,
the price of
apathy,
or inattention.
oh but the stakes
are high,
aren't they?
the highest.

ovation

a daily horror.
an errant
suspicion,
lurking.
a shadow
of thought
persistently
fleeting..
there upon
awakening ,
suddenly
in the mystic
pre-dawn,
where time
is challenged
and reason
bested.
another
unwelcome
confirmation,

formless
and haunting,
a hint
of death,
a terrible
fear
that something
vital
has been
forgotten.

the threat
of memory
too dark
to bear
suddenly
rearing its head

brandishing
its horns

angry with
an uncomfortable
observation

tired of these
inherited
myths

slither
away

lost and weary
peering at the
audience of
my own multitudes
deafened by their
acrimonious
applause

the line

there in the line
a woman
I can have,
a scripture
I can use

there
 - in the break
one word
beneath
the next

a little god
seeps in
what
a fucking
miracle

as the days
collect
like old
receipts,
a fiver found
in a jacket
a baggie
hiding
in an old
pair of jeans

like that

simple words
sitting down
near the water

finally
a quiet place
to shed

costume
clothes
and serenity
blankets
inside
where
stories
fold

there in the lines

something to
whisper to
when the night
quiets

prayer enough
I suppose
nothing cleaner
will ever
find me

the cadence
of space
like blues notes
hanging
heavy
on the wind

little redemptions
falling in line

a woman in heals
clicking toward me
one foot leaning
a little more
into the street
than the other
and the sky
might as well

break open
for all that does

the storm of sex
like lightning
striking down

deep into
my cells

it's there
it's all there

waiting

in the line

the space
between
all we forget
and everything
we know

the space
between

holding on

and

letting go.

testimony

crip walking,
high stepping,
sidewalk tripping,
all Escher stairs
and
geometry ssslipppin.

I didn't know
you fucked
with that shit,
how much
you got?

sinking into
the couch
working at the
cup of
miso soup
and shrooms

and some pull
from the core,
the center
of something

vegetable mind
and the hive
behind

all that

helicopters
and crack kibbles
on the rug
sweats and
pulling the curtains
tight

something's out
there,
something's
in here.

turn the little
lamp on.
watch your
breathing.
damn.
that weed
is strong,
that medicinal
medical is
something else

that cave
thing
in Africa

I was trying
to tell you
about
the plant
magic and
the old finger
medicine

hurling
over banisters,
into bowls
near rivers,
tiny fires

remember

some cellular
inheritance
long suspected,
leaning into

the steering wheel
sliding down
into the seat
of the car

I was starting
to tell you

remember

the dark dream,
visionary slur
with marble
columns,
and some volcanic
river of black,
the checkered
floors

remember

you were so
happy that you
could call it
vapor
all that you
ever were
had become
vapor
and you kept
rolling the word
around
on your tongue
vapor, va por
VAY-POUR

and then
your
tiny toast
of words,

your two
dimensional
exaltation

remember

weeping
because
you couldn't
describe it
and all the
words were just
missing
the point.
weeping
because
you didn't want
to forget.
but you
didn't
and you're
still here
to speak
on it
to testify.
you're still
here
and it's not
for nothing.
it's for a reason,
you're
for a reason.

The End

for
Henry P. Cruz

Dennis Cruz has been writing and performing his poetry for over 20 years. Born in Costa Rica and brought to the United States as a young boy, he inhabits the voice of the perpetual outsider and the purely American dissident. Cruz is the author of *No One: Poems 2009* and *Moth Wing Tea.* He has been published in numerous anthologies as well as online publications including *THE CHIRON REVIEW, The Nervous Breakdown, Crush Fan Zine,* and *Sensitive Skin* Magazine. He has lectured at the USC Community Literature Initiative, the Harvard-Westlake preparatory school, as well as the LA County Jail for men and women. He was also selected as one of the newer poets to watch in 2009 by the ALOUD series at the Los Angeles Public Library. He lives in Northeast Los Angeles with his wife and son.

Praise for The Beast is We

In *The Beast is We,* Dennis Cruz masterfully pulls the mattress sheet back, exposing a host of traumatizing events that takes us inside the mind of a survivor-child, reeking from the barrel of humanity like a beer bottle spilled over a bed. *The Beast is We,* takes us to the underbelly of Los Angeles, where hookers seem too tender to touch and men have stabbed their own children inside SUVs. This poetry is an oral argument or verbal graffiti, where the poet is victor, accomplice and victim. Brutal, edgy, unapologetically raw and in your face, Cruz takes us so dangerously close to the brink we all end up with "someone else's blood on our hands."

- Pam Ward
author of *Want Some Get Some*
and *Bad Girls Burn Slow*

If perspective can be defined as the interrelation in which a subject or its parts are mentally viewed, then this collection is a testament to Cruz's ability to see and poetically articulate the grime that we sweep under the rug, or the piss-stained part of life that our subconscious buries, knowing full well that acknowledgement would certainly choke us to death. This book is courageous and unapologetic in its rawness-its peeling back of the skin we lay over life's hideous blood and muscle.

Cruz's The Beast is We is proof that debauchery can be eloquent-that a pearl necklace can be fashioned from pain and curse words. Inscribing the horrors of existence with his eyes wide open and his middle fingers raised, Dennis Cruz is one of the best writers Los Angeles has ever produced

- Hiram Sims
Professor USC
Executive Director of the Community Literature Initiative USC

Dennis Cruz is one of those writers that you don't want to have to follow at a live reading. But he's more than an amazing stage presence. Haunted by profound personal loss and the specter of addiction, he draws us into his dark world where the only consolation is "there is no / winning./ only / different / takes / on the same defeat." THE BEAST IS WE is a testament to a hard-lived life. Cruz's caged beast sings a sickening blues as he takes us on a journey through drugs, whores, suicide, abandonment, aging, fatherhood, and eroticism. Sometimes a little god seeps in, sometimes he chooses Carver over Christ, and sometimes he finds grace in the ordinary. Trigger warning snowflakes: change out of your pajamas, down a shot, take a hit, and dig in.

- Wendy Rainey
Author of *Hollywood Church: Short Stories and Poems*
Contributing Poetry Editor, Chiron Review.

All I know about poetry is what talks to me and Dennis Cruz's work screams my name. His poems are about those hidden familiar secrets, that darkness inside of us, our screwed up families, that crazy kid you used to know, your long lost friends, weird strangers, and all the insanity in between. His prose is so intensely intimate I know him like the brother I always wanted. He had me with *Moth Wing Tea,* now he's kicking even more ass with *The Beast Is We*. Why the hell Dennis Cruz isn't Los Angeles' Poet Laureate I have no idea, but he's got my vote. Buy this book or you're dead to me.

- Patrick O'neil
Author of *Gun, Needle, Spoon*

OTHER PUNK HOSTAGE PRESS BOOKS

FRACTURED (2012) by Danny Baker

BETTER THAN A GUN IN A KNIFE FIGHT (2012) by A. Razor

THE DAUGHTERS OF BASTARDS (2012) by Iris Berry

DRAWN BLOOD: COLLECTED WORKS FROM D.B.P.LTD., 1985-1995 (2012) by A. Razor

IMPRESS (2012) by C.V. Auchterlonie

TOMORROW, YVONNE - POETRY & PROSE FOR SUICIDAL EGOISTS (2012) by Yvonne De la Vega

BEATEN UP BEATEN DOWN (2012) by A. Razor

MIRACLES OF THE BLOG: A SERIES (2012) by Carolyn Srygley-Moore

8TH & AGONY (2012) by Rich Ferguson

SMALL CATASTROPHES IN A BIG WORLD (2012) by A. Razor

UNTAMED (2013) by Jack Grisham

MOTH WING TEA (2013) by Dennis Cruz

HALF-CENTURY STATUS (2013) by A. Razor

SHOWGIRL CONFIDENTIAL (2013) by Pleasant Gehman

BLOOD MUSIC (2013) by Frank Reardon

I WILL ALWAYS BE YOUR WHORE/LOVE SONGS FOR BILLY CORGAN (2014) by Alexandra Naughton

HISTORY OF BROKEN LOVE THINGS (2014) by SB Stokes

YEAH, WELL... (2014) by Joel Landmine

DREAMS GONE MAD WITH HOPE (2014) by S.A. Griffin

CODE BLUE: A LOVE STORY (2014) by Jack Grisham

HOW TO TAKE A BULLET AND OTHER SURVIVAL POEMS (2014) by Hollie Hardy

DEAD LIONS (2014) by A.D. Winans

SCARS (2014) by Nadia Bruce-Rawlings

STEALING THE MIDNIGHT FROM A HANDFUL OF DAYS (2014) by Michele McDannold

WHEN I WAS A DYNAMITER, Or, How a Nice Catholic Boy Became a Merry Prankster, a Pornographer, and a Bridegroom Seven Times (2104) by Lee Quarnstrom

THUGSNESS AS A VIRTUE (2014) by Hannah Wehr

DAYS OF XMAS POEMS (2014) by A. Razor

INTROVERT/EXTROVERT (2015) by Russell Jaffe

YOU COULD NEVER OBJECTIFY ME MORE THAN I'VE ALREADY OBJECTIFIED MYSELF (2015) by Alexandra Naughton

NO GREATER LOVE (2015) by Die Dragonetti

NO PARACHUTES TO CARRY ME HOME (2015) by Maisha Z Johnson

#1 SON AND OTHER STORIES (2017) by Michael Marcus

LOOKING FOR JOHNNY, THE LEGEND OF JOHNNY THUNDERS by Danny Garcia (2018)